Sewing Stylish Home Projects

Over 30 Accessories for Your Home

LINDA LEE

The Taunton Press

Publisher: Jim Childs

Acquisitions Editor: Jolynn Gower

Assistant Editor: Sarah Coe

Copy Editor: Diane Sinitsky

Cover and Interior Designer: Lori Wendin

Layout Artist: Lori Wendin

Photographer: Jack Deutsch

Photo Stylists: Joe Bussell and Linda Lee

Illustrator: Christine Ericson

Taunton
BOOKS & VIDEOS
for fellow enthusiasts

Printed in the United States of America

10 9 8 7 6 5 4 3 2 1

The Taunton Press, Inc., 63 South Main Street,
PO Box 5506, Newtown, CT 06470-5506

e-mail: tp@taunton.com

Distributed by Publishers Group West

Library of Congress Cataloging-in-Publication Data

Lee, Linda, 1948-
Sewing stylish home projects : over 30 accessories
for your home / Linda Lee.
p.   cm.
ISBN 1-56158-337-5
1. Household linens. 2. Textile fabrics in interior decoration.
3. Machine sewing. 4. Title.
TT387.L44   2001
646.2'1—dc21   00-057724

To my daughter, Alexandra, who is immensely creative and talented. And I love her very much.

W acknowledgments

When I was growing up, my mother's friends would question her sanity for letting me use the sewing machine. Wouldn't I run a needle through my finger? My mother's answer was simply that if I did, she would pull it out, and "Wasn't riding a tricycle on a brick sidewalk more dangerous?" My mother let me sew on the best sewing machine she could afford, use any fabric in the house, and pretty much "have at it" anytime. I thank her for that freedom and encouragement. Now I make her clothes, and she has forgotten that she ever sewed.

I grew up watching my father operate a linotype. I remember his ink-stained hands gliding over the keyboard and efficiently manipulating hand type. I believe that you are born with particular hand skills. I got my feel for cloth and ability to manipulate fabric from my dad. I think of him as I watch my hands.

This book has been rattling around in my head for a few years. Jolynn Gower, an acquisitions editor at The Taunton Press, was the one who finally liked the idea. Without her there would be no book. She was open to the concept and stayed with it through all the metamorphoses. Her counseling was invaluable.

The room settings were an important ingredient in the presentation of this book. I want to thank my good friends in Topeka, Kansas, for the use of their homes both before and during the photo shoot. Tim and Jett

Elmer let us totally take over their house and disrupt their cats, even while they were out of the country. Marge Barry stood by and watched as we moved every piece of furniture and accessory in her dining room and changed the beautiful setting that she already had. Don Barry was smart to stay away that day.

Dea and Keith Olson let us invade their home during the Christmas season. We set the beautiful holiday decorations aside and went to work. The incredible lifetime collection of authentic Americana furniture and accessories was a real asset to this project. Thank you so very much.

No photo shoot can ever be as smooth as when I have the privilege of working with Jack Deutsch. He has the ultimate patience, and I have come to rely on his creative instincts, too. I hope I will have many more reasons to work with him again.

My sewing mentor is Dort Johnson. She taught me just about everything I know about sewing. She is the best stitcher and the most creative person I know. Thanks to her for sharing her knowledge and encouraging me along the way.

And special thanks to my husband, Craig, who never complains about my nonstop commitments and workload. I don't know that he completely understands why I do what I do, but he has never said "no." Thank you for your loving support.

CONTENTS

Introduction 2

CHAPTER 1
Modern Country Bedroom 6

Suspender Clipped Panels 12
Grosgrain-Trimmed Pillow 15
Journal Cover 17
Jumbo Bed Rolls 20
Lap Quilt 23
Quilted Shams 26
Sachets 29
Boudoir Pillow 31
Small Bed Roll 34
Grosgrain Fringe Pillow 36

CHAPTER 2
Victorian Parlor Charm 38

Cocard Tieback 44
Scallop Flange Pillow 48
Fragments and Fringe Pillow 52
Lampshade Slipcover 55
Silk and Lace Throw 58
Inverted Pleat Slipcover 61
Tuffet 65
Octagonal Table Topper 68
Crinkled Table Skirt 72

CHAPTER 3
Asian Dining Room 74

Kimono Border Table Runner 80
Pagoda Place Mats 83
Monogram Napkin 85
Beaded Napkin Ring 87
Shoji Slipcover 89
Japanese Tea Cozies 92

CHAPTER 4
Americana Family Room 96

Autumn Afghan 102
Basket Liner 106
Fringed Pillow 108
Laced Pillow 111
Mantel Cover 114
Stenciled Table Cover 117

CHAPTER 5
The Basics for Sewing 120

Resources 140

introduction

I have been a practicing interior designer for 30 years and a hobby sewer for many more years than that. For most of those 30 years, I simply designed the various products that I used in my clients' homes such as pillows, drapery treatments, and table covers. I designed them on paper, but I did not make them. I never gave that aspect a thought. The engineering of how to construct something was why you took the ideas and the materials to an interior sewing workroom. I was never taught how to make anything in design school. And the subject of sewing was never approached.

In 1993, I purchased the Sewing Workshop in San Francisco. One of the first phone calls I received was from one of the big pattern companies, asking me if I would be the content editor, sample maker, and scriptwriter for a PBS television series called *Sewing Today*. Of the 27 shows to be written, about one-third of them featured sewing for interiors. Suddenly, I was thrown into the world of having to figure out how to make things that I had never made. I was soon making ribbon-woven table skirts, tailored linen roman shades, ruffled pillow shams, and insulated place mats and napkins.

Soon after I was involved in the sample making and technical writing for two books on interior decorating products—pillows and slipcovers. The deadline was so fierce on both projects that I ended up making most of the projects myself so that I would completely understand how they were made and I would know how to write the copy.

I was getting my feet wet in a hurry. My learning curve was huge, but I was enjoying every minute of it. After the dust had settled on these projects, I became aware that this was where the sewing industry was headed with a new marketing emphasis on home decorating. My design background and my knowledge of the inside of the interior design world plus my sewing skills borrowed from fashion sewing were a perfect combination. I knew I wanted to make things for my own home and for my clients.

At first glance, there seems to be a separation of fabrics available for use for the sewing industry and for the interior design industry. Sewers think that only fabrics they see in the retail fabric stores, which also tend to be discount stores, are available to them. But there is a huge world of incredible fabrics that are available "to

the trade" only, meaning that only interior designers can order them. But a common misconception is that interior designers will not deal with a client who is interested in ordering fabric only. In fact, you can go into a designer's sample room, work with or without the designer to find what you want, and order yardage in any quantity that you need. Of course, you may be on your own to figure out the bugs in making your project work, or you may be able to pay the designer a fee to assist you in the mechanics of making the item.

As a sewer who has been primarily interested in learning couture sewing techniques, I have been able to blend the fine details and strong dressmaking skills into better sewing for my interior design clients. On two different occasions, I used two workrooms to make things that had mitered corners—one was a bordered

table runner and the others were sheer window panels. Upon inspecting the final products, I noticed that the corners on both pieces were sloppy and not really sewn, only pressed to simulate a miter. That's when I realized that workrooms do not always know the precision details that we, as fashion sewers, have worked so hard to learn and perfect.

I have also noticed a trend in home interiors of using fabrics that have been traditionally used in fashion, such as silk dupioni, silk organza, silk charmeuse, and handkerchief linen. The good news for us is that these fabrics are more readily available in better fabric stores across the country, they are less expensive than their cousins as ordered by interior designers, and they are more manageable on our home sewing machines. And of course, they are so luscious. Heavy cut velvets and tapestries with thick latex backings take a lot more effort to wrestle around your sewing room, and some home sewing machines are not suited to sewing these fabrics.

This book is designed to integrate good sewing techniques and materials borrowed from the fashion industry and to introduce them into sewing for your home. The projects are manageable with relatively small amounts of materials, and you can accomplish them in a short time. This book is about taking an already rather complete room and adding personality, character, and polish. Your touches will define the house and who lives there.

It's rare that we want to take on the project of making large quantities of draperies for our homes. It takes a lot of fabric, enormous table space, and specialized equipment. Plus, it is not all that creative. But imagine the creativity in planning and making just the beautiful tiebacks.

Upholstering a chair requires a hammer and nails and some brute strength. A simple slipcover, made with fabric, needle, and thread, changes a chair instantly, and you can do it yourself. Pillows are the new artistic accessory. Mail-order catalogs, magazines, and every imaginable kind of store (I've even seen them in the grocery store) show them for every reason and season. And some of them cost a fortune. Pillows are the easiest way to use beautiful fabrics, combine them in interesting ways, and add some exotic trims. Pillows provide the canvas for playing. Throw them on a tired sofa, and it is rejuvenated.

Dining table accessories are pretty ordinary in the stores. And have you ever really found the perfect color to use with your dishes anyway? Splurge on a great piece of fabric, and sew a place mat in a new and interesting shape. Add a napkin with a satin monogram, and trim it with a piece of jewelry as a napkin ring.

Shop in your own stash of fabrics. You will be surprised to find how many fabrics you own that you would not actually wear as a garment but that might be perfect for your home. Don't save them for the next special occasion that never comes. Use them now!

I hope that this book will inspire you to look at your home with a new eye and see how you can update the look with small handmade accessories.

MODERN COUNTRY BEDROOM

modern
country bedroom

WE ALL HAVE A VISION of a retreat—a place to go for peace and serenity. Some can go to the hills of Tuscany, some to a weekend studio outside of a bustling city, others to a fishing cabin near the river. For most of us, our bedroom is the only possibility. One way or another we create a private room away from the world.

Sometimes bedrooms are planned. Designers are hired; the right look is purchased; things are ordered and delivered. Sometimes they just happen. Furniture and stuff is moved into the room, and little planning takes place. "We'll do the room when the kids are gone."

But maybe the retreat can happen without the need to "do the room." Work with the family worn bedspread. Add some great pillows—lots of them, oversized and squishy. Use some fabrics and textures that you don't normally think of using together, such as linen with organza. Think about leaning against some quilted pillows, reading a book, with your feet nestled under a

A basic room with oak flooring, plain walls, and an eclectic mixture of pine and painted furniture provides a simple background for beautiful sewing projects. Pillows in various sizes and shapes, a luxurious lap quilt, simple drapery panels, a journal cover, and some sachets in crisp summery fabrics and soft tones finish the setting and add personality.

Strong color, pattern, and texture add a bold statement. These hot Mexican and southwestern colors of the earth and sky are uniquely combined in broad stripes, small dots, leafy shapes, and rough textures. Transpose these fabrics and colors into the previous setting and you can see in the illustration on the facing page how everything changes.

thick but light-as-a-feather lap quilt. Have your exquis-itely covered journal handy, pencil ready. Freshen the air with flowers and fragrance.

This bedroom is a real getaway, reminiscent of the countryside in the summer with cool breezes and mid-day sunshine. French country pine in a mellow hue is a wonderful contrast to the pale tones of handkerchief linen, silk dupioni, and organza. Casual, slightly wrin-kled and natural, down-filled bedcovers and pillows are now the standard for everyday bed dressing. Add the small details, letting your imagination run free, and settle in for a wonderful nap.

By simply changing the fabrications, the same projects in a different room can look completely different. The original French country look gives way to an even more casual look combining wrought iron, wicker and rattan, and rag rugs. More color and pattern help to "fill" the room visually.

suspender clipped panels

FINISHED SIZE: *VARIABLE*

« materials

Fabric

1-in.-wide grosgrain ribbon

(see Resources on p. 140)

Suspender clips

Thread to match

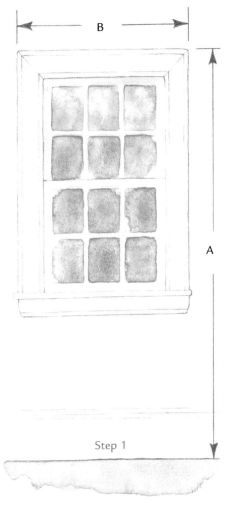

B

A

Step 1

UNLINED PANELS ARE MADE from a clipped-weave Indian cotton (see Resources on p. 140). The tops are folded and draped loosely to form a soft, flounced heading. In this variation of a tab-top drapery, strips of grosgrain ribbon loop through suspender clips that attach to the top of the flounce about every 6 in. Each panel in the sample project is one width of fabric and extends from the top of the window frame to the floor. Nothing could be simpler!

preparation

1 To determine the length of the drapery panels, measure from the top of the window frame to the floor and subtract $1/2$ in. (see A in the illustration). Add $16^1/2$ in. for the top flounce and 4 in. for the hem.

2 To determine the width, measure the width of the window from the outside of the frame to the outside of the frame (see B in the illustration). Multiply this measurement by 2.5, then divide in half and add 4 in. for side hems. Seam widths of fabric together if needed. Make two panels for each window.

3 For the tabs, cut 7-in.-long strips of grosgrain ribbon. Cut enough to place them approximately every 6 in. along the width of each panel.

✱ Choose a fabric that is attractive on both the right and wrong sides. The wrong side of the fabric will show at the top flounce.

✴ When installing the panels on a rod, arrange the tabs about 2 in. apart so that the flounce will drape and fall irregularly. Even though the panels can be pulled to open and close, consider installing blinds or shades under them for privacy so that you can leave the panels as window dressing only.

✴ Drapery hardware is readily available in myriad sizes and finishes. Whether using metal, wood, or composite materials, make sure that the loop tab is significantly larger than the diameter of the rod.

construction

① Press 1 in. to the wrong side of each panel side edge. Fold again to make 1-in. finished hems, then topstitch, machine-blindstitch, or hand-slipstitch.

② Following step 1 for the side hems, make 2-in. double hems at the bottom of each panel.

③ Turn ½ in. to the right side at the top of each panel, then fold the top 8 in. to the right side. Topstitch at the ½-in. folded edge. To encourage a soft, flounced look, do not press the top fold.

Step 3

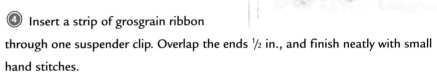

④ Insert a strip of grosgrain ribbon through one suspender clip. Overlap the ends ½ in., and finish neatly with small hand stitches.

⑤ Finally, fold the top of each panel along the topstitching line to the right side. Attach the suspender clips to the fold about 6 in. apart.

Step 4   Step 5

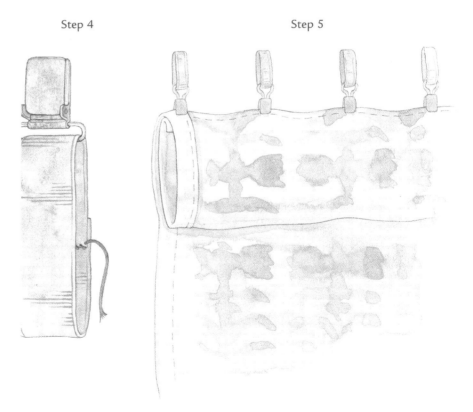

grosgrain-trimmed pillow

THIS SMALL, decorative pillow has the normally back, overlapping closure as its featured detail on the front. The pillow combines plaid silk dupioni with two colors of handkerchief linen. Grosgrain ribbon loops decorate the overlapping band.

FINISHED SIZE: 12 IN. BY 16 IN.

« materials

Fabrics
- 1½ yd. fabric for basic pillow
- ¼ yd. fabric for side trim
- ¼ yd. fabric for overlap band

1 yd. of ½-in.-wide grosgrain
  ribbon (see Resources on p. 140)
Thread to match
One 12-in. by 16-in. pillow form
  (see Resources on p. 140)

preparation

① Using the fabric for the basic pillow, cut one piece 13 in. by 15½ in. for the front and cut one piece 13 in. by 17 in. for the back.

② Cut one piece 5 in. by 13 in. for the side trim.

③ For the overlap band, cut one piece 6 in. by 13 in.

④ From the grosgrain ribbon, cut seven pieces 4¼ in. long.

Step 2

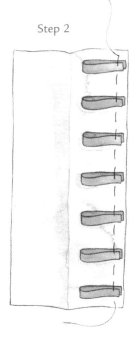

construction

① Fold the overlap band in half lengthwise with the wrong sides together and press.

② Next, fold each piece of ribbon in half to form a loop. Aligning the raw edges, evenly space the ribbon loops along one edge of the overlap band. Start and end the loops about ½ in. inside the seam allowances, then baste in place.

Step 3

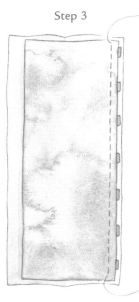

③ With right sides together, sew the side trim piece to the trimmed edge of the overlap band. Trim the seam and press it toward the side trim.

④ Serge-finish one short end of the basic pillow front, then turn the finished end to the wrong side 2½ in. and topstitch.

⑤ Pin the overlap band over the front hem and baste together.

⑥ With right sides together, sew the pillow front to the pillow back.

⑦ Turn the pillow to the outside, then insert the form between the overlap band and the front.

Step 4

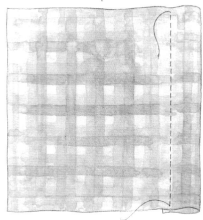

making square corners

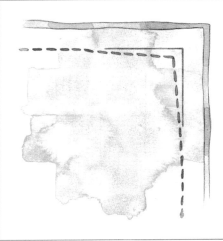

WHEN THE PILLOW FORM is inserted into your pillow, the corner is distorted. The following technique adjusts the seam so that the corners look square.

1. Draw a seam allowance along each side of the fabric identifying each corner point.

2. Next, divide each edge into quarters. Mark the quarters immediately preceding and following the corner point, then relocate the point so that it is centered at least ⅛ in. inside your original seamline.

3. As you sew the edge seam, taper the seam inward at the quarter mark immediately preceding the corner point.

journal cover

FINISHED SIZE: *8½ IN. BY 10 IN.*

T HIS JOURNAL OR BOOK COVER is a combination of materials and techniques borrowed from other projects in this chapter. The base cover is made from handkerchief linen with a pieced section of handkerchief linen and plaid silk dupioni. The dupioni is also used as a lining. A small loop of grosgrain ribbon extends from a seam to hold small scissors. A silk organza sheer overlay, serge-finished with rayon decorative thread, is stitched down to form six pockets for pencils. The journal size used is 8½ in. by 10 in. The fabric is secured to the book covers with 5-in.-wide facings.

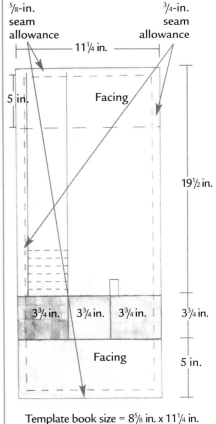

≪ materials

Fabrics

- ⅜ yd. basic fabric
- ⅛ yd. of three contrasting fabrics
- ⅛ yd. sheer fabric
- ⅜ yd. fusible interfacing
- ½ yd. of 1-in.-wide grosgrain ribbon (see Resources on p. 140)

Thread to match

- Three spools rayon decorative or 100% silk (see Resources on p. 140)
- One spool cotton or polyester

Template for the sample project (see the illustration below)

⅝-in. seam allowance

¾-in. seam allowance

11¼ in.

5 in.   Facing

19½ in.

3¾ in.   3¾ in.   3¾ in.   3¾ in.

Facing   5 in.

Template book size = 8⅝ in. x 11¼ in.

preparation

① For the basic cover, cut one piece of fabric 13 in. by 20½ in. and one piece 13 in. by 6 in.

② For the lining, cut one piece of fabric 13 in. by 12 in.

③ For the pieced section, cut three pieces 4¼ in. by 4¼ in. from each of the contrasting fabrics.

④ Cut one piece 3¾ in. by 20⅛ in. from the sheer fabric.

⑤ From the grosgrain ribbon, cut one piece 4 in. for the scissors loop and one piece 14 in. for the bookmark.

construction

① With right sides together, stitch the three pieces for the pieced section together to make one long strip. Press the seams open.

② Using matching rayon decorative thread or silk thread, serge-finish the two long edges of the sheer fabric.

③ Fold the short piece of ribbon in half to form a loop. Aligning the raw edges, baste the loop to the bottom corner of the top section of the pieced strip. Also matching raw edges, baste the sheer piece to the bottom pieced section, aligning the top edge of the sheer with the seam and keeping it out of the seam allowance of the cover.

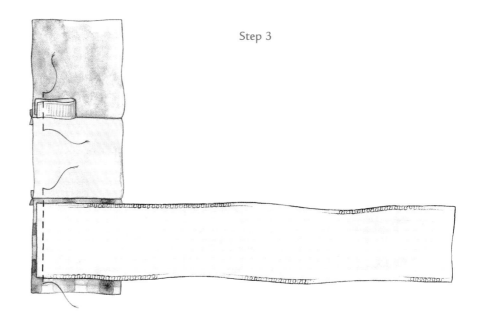

Step 3

④ With right sides together, sew one short edge of the basic cover to the basted edge of the pieced section.

Step 5

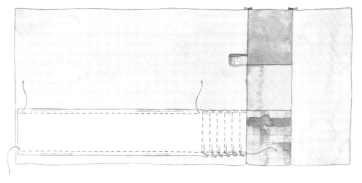

⑤ To the left of the bottom pieced section, draw six vertical lines ⅝ in. apart on the basic cover. On the sheer fabric, mark lines ¾ in. apart. Align the markings to form small pencil pockets, then stitch through the markings the entire height of the sheer fabric. At the bottom of each pocket, pin small tucks. Edgestitch along the bottom of the sheer strip, continuing through the pockets, then edgestitch across the top of the sheer, stopping at the beginning of the pockets.

6 Serge-finish the ends of the cover, including catching the sheer strip on one end.

7 Aligning the raw edges, pin the ribbon bookmark to the right side of the top edge of the cover just to the left of the center of the back cover. Fold the underlap facings to the right side along the foldlines, then center the lining over the cover and facings. The lining will cover the facings by about 2 in. Stitch $\frac{1}{2}$-in. seam allowances across the top and bottom. At the bottom, stitch on the side of the previous stitching so as not to catch the sheer strip in the stitching.

8 Turn the cover to the outside and insert the journal.

✳ It is better to make the cover too loose rather than too tight, so your measurements can be generous.

Step 7

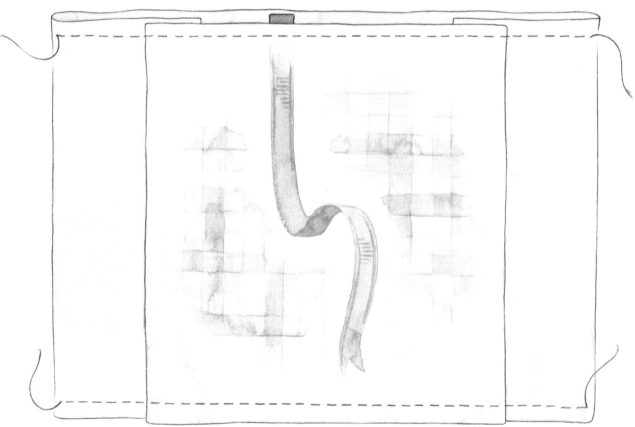

✳ To calculate the basic cover size for any journal, use the following formula. For the width, measure the width of the journal times two plus the thickness and 10 in. for two underlap facings, then add the seam allowances. For the height, measure the height of the journal plus $1\frac{3}{4}$ in. for the seam allowances and the thickness of the cover.

jumbo bed rolls

FINISHED SIZE: 38 IN. BY 10 IN. DIA.

<< **materials**

Fabrics

- 2¼ yd. for two bed rolls
- 1 yd. for welting for two bed rolls
- 2 yd. #200 cable cord

Thread to match

Two 38-in. by 10-in.-dia. feather
  and down bolster forms
  (see Resources on p. 140)

T HESE JUMBO BED ROLLS are down-filled bolsters covered with plaid silk dupioni. The welt trim at each end is handkerchief linen, a fabric borrowed from other projects in the same room setting. Two bolsters this size fit the width of a king-size bed.

cutting bias strips

1. To cut bias strips, find the straight of grain by tearing the fabric or pulling a thread.

2. Make sure the fabric is square, then measure an equal distance from the corner along each side. Draw a diagonal line connecting both points.

Step 2

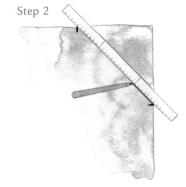

Step 3

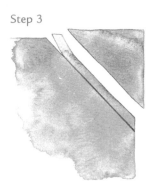

3. Measure 1½ in. from that line and mark the width of the strips, then cut.

preparation

① For the bolsters, cut two 33-in. by 39-in. pieces and cut four 11-in.-dia. circles. Use a compass to make perfect circles.

② For the welting, cut 2 yd. of 1½-in.-wide bias strips (see the sidebar at left). Wrap the bias strips around cable cord with the wrong sides together. With a zipper or cording foot, stitch close to the cord to encase it. Trim the excess fabric to create a ½-in. seam allowance.

✳ You can shorten the down bolsters a few inches without having to remove
feathers by making a fold in the outer muslin covering and hand-stitching a pleat.

✳ When sewing welting, use a cording-foot attachment on your sewing machine. The grooved cutout on the underside of the foot holds the welting in place while you sew, and by adjusting the needle placement, you can sew closer to the cord.

Step 2

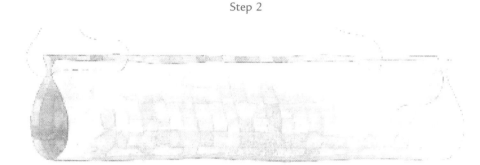

construction

 Using the bolster pieces, press the seam allowances to the wrong sides on the long edges.

② Beginning at each end, sew the long edges together for about 8 in., leaving the center open.

③ Cut the welting into four equal lengths. Matching the raw edges, sew the welting to the right side of each bolster end. Clip the flange of the welting as needed and join the ends neatly.

④ With right sides together, pin one end of the bolster to one of the round ends, clipping the bolster as needed. Repeat and pin the other end, then sew the ends to the bolster.

⑤ Turn the bolster cover right side out. Insert the down form and slipstitch the opening.

Step 3

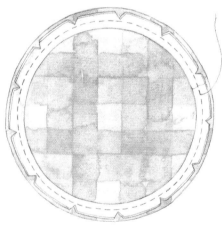

Step 4

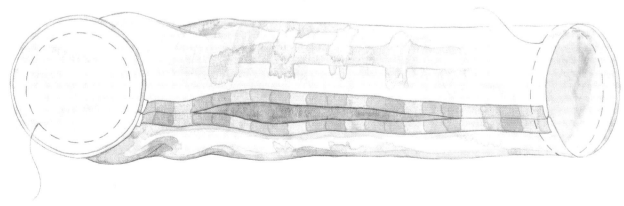

lap quilt

T HE TOP OF THIS LAP QUILT consists of nine rectangular sections of three colors of handkerchief linen. One of the colors is repeated as a solid back. Both layers are held together by fabric-covered buttons surrounded by silk organza rosettes placed at each color-block corner.

FINISHED SIZE: 54 IN. BY 62 IN.

« materials

One 54-in. by 62-in. goose-down
   lap quilt (see Resources on p. 140)

Fabrics

- Color 1: 1⅛ yd. (45-in. width)
   or ⅔ yd. (60-in. width)
- Color 2: 1⅛ yd. (45-in. width)
   or ⅔ yd. (60-in. width)
- Color 3: 4¼ yd. (45-in. width)
   or 2½ yd. (60-in. width)

Trims

- ⅛ yd. sheer fabric
- Eight 1¼-in.-dia. buttons to
   cover (see Resources on p. 140)
- ⅛ yd. contrasting fabric
   (reserved from the Jumbo Bed Roll
   project on pp. 20–22)

Thread to match

- Three spools rayon decorative
   or 100% silk (see Resources on
   p. 140)
- One spool cotton or polyester
- Cordonnet or buttonhole twist

preparation

In the following dimensions, ½-in. seam allowances are included.

① From each of the three fabric colors, cut three pieces 19 in. by 21¾ in.

② For color 3, also cut one piece 55 in. by 63 in.

③ From the sheer fabric, cut three crosswise strips 1½ in. wide for the rosettes.

④ From the contrasting fabric, cut eight 2¼-in.-dia. circles for the buttons.

Step 1

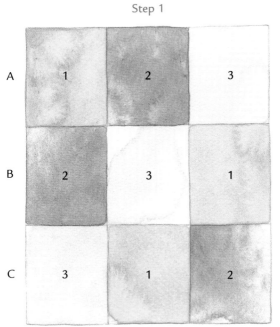

construction

① Organize the fabric rectangles according to the illustration.

② Starting with the top row A, sew one long edge of color 1 to one long edge of color 2 with right sides together. Sew the other long edge of color 2 to one long edge of color 3. Serge-finish the raw edges together, then press toward the outside edges. Sew rows B and C according to the illustration.

③ With right sides together, sew one long edge of row A to a long edge of row B. Sew the other long edge of row B to a long edge of row C. Serge-finish the raw edges together, then press the seams toward the outside edges.

④ Lay the pieced quilt top on top of the large, back piece of color 3. Trim both pieces to the same size.

⑤ Serge-finish one short end of the pieced top and the back piece. With right sides together, sew the pieced top to the back around four sides, leaving a large opening at one short end. Insert the down lap quilt, then turn the remaining seam allowances to the inside and slipstitch the opening.

Step 3

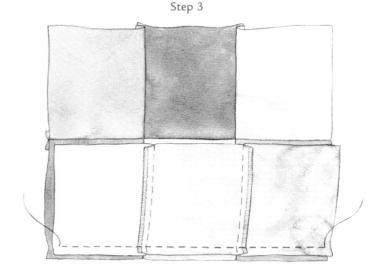

Step 5

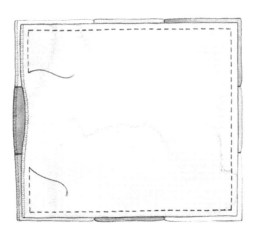

⑥ Cover the buttons with the contrasting circles.

⑦ Using a three-thread stitch formation and the decorative thread, serge-finish both of the long edges of the sheer strips, then cut into eight 12-in.-long strips.

⑧ Next, make the sheer rosettes by hand-sewing a gathering stitch along one edge of each strip. Pull up the gathers to create a ring and secure the thread. Sew the ends together neatly by hand.

✱ A similar look for this lap quilt can be achieved by using several layers of cotton batting as the filler rather than a down quilt.

Step 8

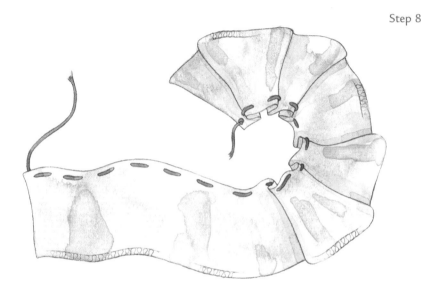

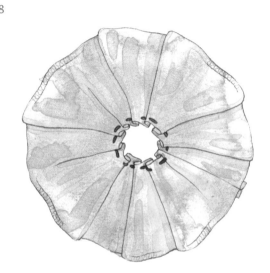

⑨ Hand-tack a rosette to each color-block corner on both sides of the quilt.

⑩ Finally, sew a covered button in the center of each rosette. Do this by threading a sturdy needle with heavy thread and inserting the needle all the way through the center of a rosette. Pull the thread through all of the layers, leaving a tail of thread on both sides, and remove the needle. Repeat about $1/4$ in. away. On one side of the quilt, tie a square knot, leaving the long thread tails hanging. Repeat on the other side, pulling the thread tight to indent the quilt. On one side of the quilt, pass one thread end through a button shank and tie securely to the other thread end. Cut off the excess threads. Repeat on the other side.

Step 10

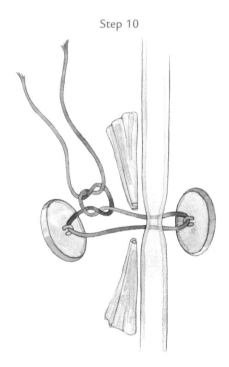

quilted shams

FINISHED SIZE: 24 IN. BY 40 IN.

<< **m a t e r i a l s**

Fabrics
- 5 yd. fabric for two shams
- 5 yd. cotton batting for two
  shams (see Resources on p. 140)

40 buttons

Thread to match
- One spool rayon decorative
  thread or 100% silk
- One spool cotton or polyester

Two 24-in. by 32-in. pillow forms

preparation

① Mark two 40-in. by 49-in. rectangles on the fabric. Cut around the rectangles, leaving a few extra inches.

② Cut two pieces of cotton batting the same size as the fabric.

THESE PILLOW SHAMS are made of handkerchief linen, which is machine-quilted in a diamond pattern on one layer of cotton batting. Each side buttons with five cufflink-style closures. With 4-in. side-button bands, the shams have a finished width of 32 in.

construction

① Pin the wrong side of the fabric to one layer of cotton batting in a grid pattern about 8 in. apart, then hand-baste as needed.

② Using a long straightedge and a chalk marker, draw 45-degree diagonal lines 4 in. apart to form diamond shapes.

③ Starting in the center of the rectangle and using rayon decorative thread, sew over the marked diagonal lines through the fabric and batting.

④ Trim the rectangles to 40 in. by 49 in., then serge-finish all raw edges.

⑤ With right sides together, sew the long edges together to form a tube. Press the seam open.

Step 3

Step 5

Step 6

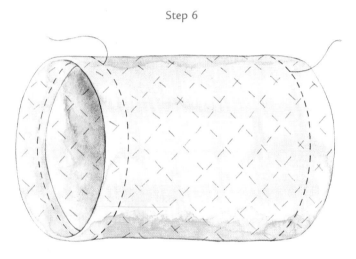

⑥ Turn 4 in. of each side to the wrong side, then topstitch 3 in. from each end.

⑦ On both the front and back of each side, make five machine buttonholes, starting each buttonhole 2 in. from the outer edge. The buttonholes on the front should line up with the buttonholes on the back.

⑧ Next, make cufflink buttons by sewing two buttons together, joining them with a 3/4-in.-long thread shank. Wax and knot a double strand of cotton or polyester thread on a needle. Starting on the underside of a button, insert the needle through one hole. Bring the needle down and through the other hole, then run the needle between the double threads above the knot to secure the threads. Insert the needle into the holes of the other button and go back and forth between the buttons several times to make a thread shank. Wrap the thread around the shank several times, pass it once through one button, and slide the needle under the wraps before knotting the thread. The length of the shank will vary depending on the thickness of your fabric.

⑨ Center a pillow form inside the sham and button the ends.

✳ Using a walking foot or an even-feed foot will prevent the fabric from creeping as it is quilted.

Step 8

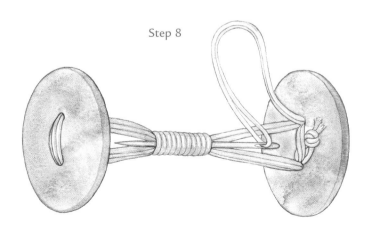

sachets

THESE SMALL, SCENTED SACHETS are made from torn, sheer organza fabrics, one side in silk organza, the other in metallic organza. Hand-stitches divide each sachet into square pockets for potpourri and finish the edges. The two divided sachets are 7 in. by 7 in., and the small sachet is 4 in. by 4 in.

FINISHED SIZES: 7 IN. BY 7 IN. AND 4 IN. BY 4 IN.

<< **m a t e r i a l s**

Fabrics
- ¼ yd. fabric for two large sachets and one small
- ¼ yd. contrasting fabric for two large sachets and one small

Pearl Crown Rayon thread

Potpourri (see Resources on p. 140)

preparation

① Tear four 7-in. by 7-in. pieces of fabric.

② Tear two 4-in. by 4-in. pieces of fabric.

✱ The torn and frayed edges are part of the sachets' design. If your fabric does not tear well, cut the edges using pinking shears or the wavy blade on a rotary cutter.

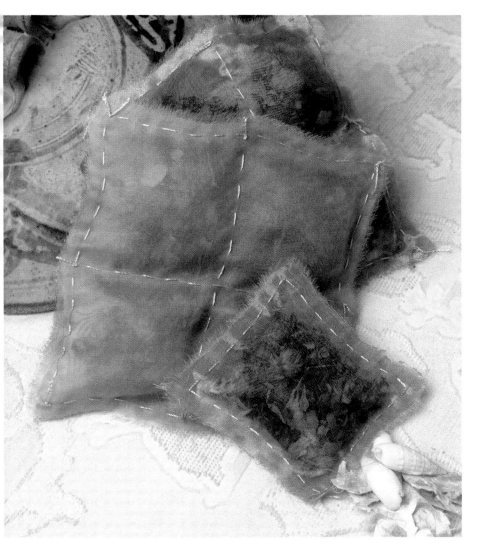

✳ Other decorative threads may be substituted for Pearl Crown Rayon. Most threads of this type tend to fray and knot up, so work with a short strand of thread at one time.

Step 2

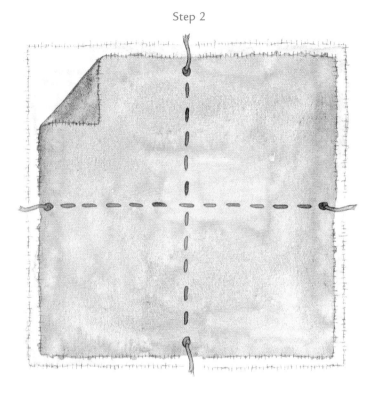

construction

① Pin the wrong side of one 7-in. by 7-in. piece of fabric to the wrong side of a contrasting piece of fabric. Draw a line from edge to edge through the center of one side. Draw another line perpendicular to the first line.

Step 4

② Knot one end of a length of Pearl Crown Rayon thread, leaving a ½-in. tail, then hand-sew a ¼-in. running stitch through each marked line. At the end of a stitching line, knot the thread and leave a tail.

③ Place a small amount of potpourri in each pocket and pin to close.

④ Next, hand-sew a running stitch around each outside edge. Begin and end the stitching at each corner, knotting the thread to start and stop.

⑤ To make a single-pocket 4-in. by 4-in. sachet, hand-sew a running stitch around the outside edges only after filling with potpourri.

boudoir pillow

FINISHED SIZE: *12 IN. BY 21 IN.*

<< materials

Fabrics
- ¹⁄₂ yd. for pillow
- ¹⁄₂ yd. for pleated ruffle

Grosgrain ribbon (see Resources on p. 140)
- ³⁄₄ yd. of 1-in.-wide ribbon
- ³⁄₄ yd. of ³⁄₈-in.-wide contrasting ribbon

Thread to match

One 12-in. by 16-in. feather and down boudoir pillow form (see Resources on p. 140)

THIS PILLOWCASE-STYLE pillow incorporates a cotton batiste print, sewn on three sides, with an inverted-pleat double ruffle at one end. A narrow grosgrain ribbon sewn to a wider piece of grosgrain embellishes the transition between the pillow and the ruffle. The down-filled boudoir pillow insert is 12 in. by 16 in., and the ruffle is 5 in. wide.

Step 1

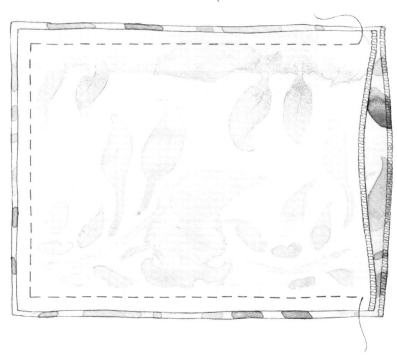

preparation

① For the pillow, cut two pieces of fabric 13 in. by 17 in.

② For the ruffle, cut one piece of fabric 10 in. by 45 in. and one piece 10 in. by 17 in.

③ From each of the grosgrain ribbons, cut one piece 25 in. long.

construction

① With right sides together, sew three sides of the pillow, leaving one short end open. Serge-finish the raw edges of the open end.

② Sew together the two pieces of the ruffle end-to-end to make one continuous strip. Fold the strip in half lengthwise with the wrong sides together and press.

③ To pleat the ruffle, mark the ruffle as follows: 1½ in., ½ in., 1 in., ½ in. Repeat this sequence the length of the ruffle, then fold the ruffle to form 1½-in.-wide inverted pleats. Baste the pleats in place and finish the raw edges together.

④ Draw a line 1 in. from the edge of the open end. Pin the ruffle on the outside of the pillow, matching the finished/raw edge to the marked line. In the center of the back, determine where the ruffle joins and mark. Sew a ¼-in. seam and cut off the excess fabric. Serge-finish and press to one side, then sew the ruffle to the pillow.

Step 3

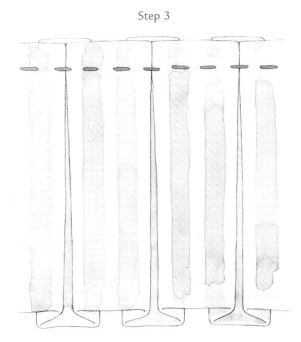

Step 4

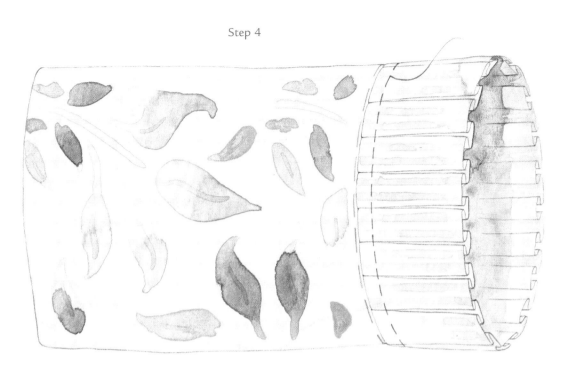

⑤ Next, center the ³⁄₈-in.-wide contrasting grosgrain ribbon on the 1-in. grosgrain. Edgestitch both sides.

⑥ Starting on the back, place the 1-in. grosgrain band slightly over the ruffle stitching line. Edgestitch both sides, then finish the ends neatly.

✳ To avoid dog-eared corners on this pillow, taper the stitching to make a wider seam allowance about 2 in. on either side of a corner.

Step 6

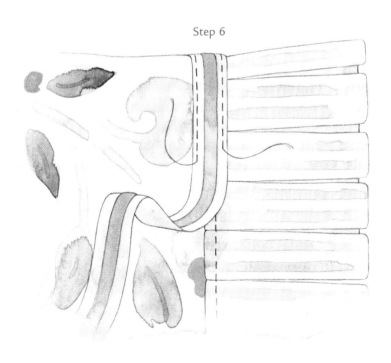

small bed roll

FINISHED SIZE: 23 IN. BY 8 IN. DIA.

<< m a t e r i a l s

Fabrics
- ⅞ yd. for pillow covering
- 1⅓ yd. sheer fabric for outer layer and facings

Trims
- ⅔ yd. ribbon
- Two pearl buckles

Thread to match
- Three spools rayon decorative or 100% silk
- One spool cotton or polyester
One 23-in. by 8-in.-dia. feather and down bed roll form (see Resources on p. 140)

✳ There is a difference in the quality of grosgrain ribbons. Look for 100% rayon grosgrain in better stores. It has more defined ribs and is slightly thicker but more pliable (see Resources on p. 140).

THE DOWN-FILLED bed roll consists of two parts. The inner covering is a loose "tube" of handkerchief linen with silk organza-faced open ends. Both ends are tied with grosgrain ribbon drawn through vintage pearl buckles. The outer layer is a loose sleeve of silk organza, serged-finished with matching rayon decorative thread and buttoned with a row of five pearl buttons. The bed roll measures 23 in. by 8 in. dia. with the inner layer extending 11 in. beyond each end.

preparation

1 For the inner covering, cut a layer of fabric the same diameter as the roll plus $\frac{1}{2}$-in. seam allowances. Cut one piece 30 in. by 46 in.

2 For the outer sleeve, cut from the sheer fabric a piece that is 1 in. larger than the diameter of the roll plus a 1-in. double hem allowance on both edges and a 1-in. underlap. Cut another piece from the sheer fabric that is 30 in. by 46 in. for the sleeve facings. These facings are cut long enough to extend about 2 in. beyond the ends of the form. Cut two pieces 23 in. by 13$\frac{1}{2}$ in. for facings.

3 For the grosgrain ties, cut two pieces 12 in. long.

Step 1

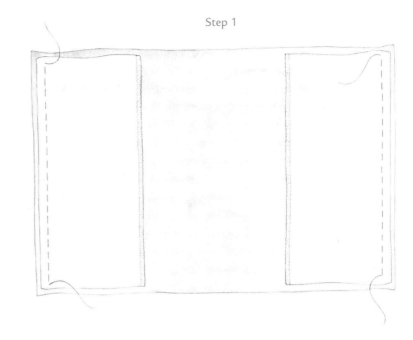

construction

1 Serge-finish one long edge of each facing. With right sides together, sew the facings to each short end of the linen body. Trim the seam and press open.

2 With the facings away from the body, sew together the long edges of the pillow, and press the seam open. Fold the facings to the inside and press, then insert the down form. The facings remain loose inside the tube.

3 Next, make two ties. Insert one end of a piece of grosgrain through a pearl buckle, wrapping it around the center about $\frac{3}{4}$ in. Turn the raw edge under and hand-stitch together, forming a loop.

4 Wrap a tie around each end of the pillow, then secure the buckle and trim the end of the ribbon in a V shape. Casually turn the ends of the facings to the outside.

Step 2

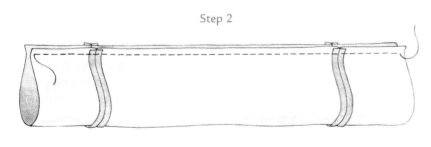

Step 3

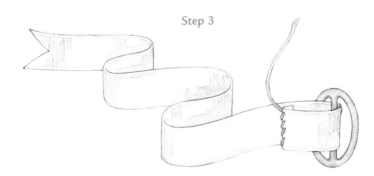

grosgrain fringe pillow

FINISHED SIZE: 12 IN. BY 16 IN.

<< materials

½ yd. linen

4 yd. of 1-in.-wide grosgrain
    ribbon (see Resources on p. 140)

One 16-in.-square pillow form

THIS SIMPLE RECTANGULAR PILLOW is made of medium-weight linen. Pieces of 1-in.-wide grosgrain ribbon, softly folded, are spaced about ½ in. apart, creating a clever fringe on all four sides. The pillow is closed with a basic slipstitched closure for the cleanest look possible.

Step 2

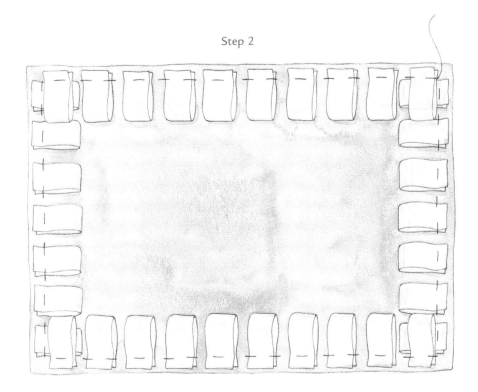

preparation

① Cut two pieces of linen 13 in. by 17 in.

② Cut 34 pieces of ribbon 4 in. long.

✴ Open one side of the pillow form and remove enough stuffing so that the pillow will measure 12 in. by 16 in. Resew the side, then cut off the excess fabric.

construction

① Fold each ribbon strip in half and pin. Do not press.

② Matching the raw edges of the ribbon pieces to the outer raw edge of the right side of one pillow piece, pin 7 ribbons to each end and 10 ribbons along the sides. Allow about ½ in. between each ribbon. Baste in place along the seamline.

③ Place the remaining pillow piece on top of the ribbon/pillow piece with right sides together. Sew around all edges, leaving an opening along one side .

④ Turn to the outside and insert the pillow form, then slipstitch the opening.

Step 3

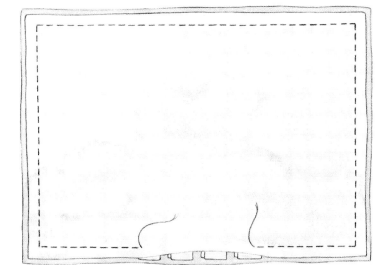

VICTORIAN PARLOR CHARM

CHAPTER 2

Victorian
parlor charm

WHATEVER HAPPENED to parlors? Were they too stuffy, too small, too forgotten? The parlor has given way to enormous family rooms with chairs and sofas, clustered mostly around a very large television. The parlor of yesterday was a place for receiving and entertaining visitors, but today's parlor provides a refuge for quiet reflection and intimate conversations.

The Victorian era was steeped with the richness of detail. Heavily textured sofas with curved edges and fringe, intricately designed chairs with inlay and carving and rugs, and draped tables of lace and tassels were the mode of the day. Colors were intense, patterns were mixed, and the word "ornate" was an understatement.

This elegant parlor setting blends all of the elements of classic Victorian with the best in new materials. New tapestry fabrics combined with new loopy fringes and rosettes on a soft, down-filled pillow are made to last and made to look old. A delightful slipcover, utilizing just a modest amount of a newly produced, historical

The classic Victorian parlor shown here is steeped in turn-of-the-century elements—the rich Chinese rug, heavy velvet and fringed settee, rare and exotic chair, and curved windows dressed in lace. But new materials and sewn projects can modernize the room while still keeping the integrity of the era. The crinkled metallic silk skirt paired with a pieced silk table topper, a trimmed and tasseled tapestry ottoman, a simple skirted slipcover, pillows, tiebacks, and a luxurious lace and satin throw add personal touches to this room.

The traditionally deep colors of Victorian interiors can be shifted to a softer, more pastel palette for a more updated look and lighter feeling, as shown in the illustration on the facing page. The black background tapestry gives way to a textured woven damask in a muted green, white linen replaces lace, whisper peach silk taffeta stands in for crinkled silk, and small prints and plaids are used in pillows and other accessories.

documentary fabric, covers just the chair seat while maintaining the most obvious charm of the chair—the back. An old crystal lamp, with a hard-to-replace lampshade, gets a facelift with a taffeta-trimmed lace slipcover. The standard off-the-rack lace curtains get upgraded with a cocard, a design borrowed from an old French hat embellishment. And the bargain, flea-market table gets covered with a crinkled "ball-gown" petticoat and a pieced silk, handkerchief tablecloth. Prop your feet on the tuffet, and take it easy in the spirit of days gone by.

Crisp linen and dupioni silk, narrow striped moire, tone-on-tone damask, and small prints in pale tones of peach and green create a beautifully formal look in this restyled parlor. The same projects, worked in different colors and fabrics, can work when using an Aubusson style rug, curved French sofa, and a straightforward chair. A folding screen and new accessories complement the setting.

cocard tieback

FINISHED SIZE: 16 IN. BY 4½ IN. DIA.

« materials

2 yd. of 1½-in.-wide grosgrain
   ribbon (see Resources on p. 140)

1¾ yd. of 1-in.-wide grosgrain
   ribbon (see Resources on p. 140)

¼ yd. of 1½-in.-wide iridescent
   silk ribbon

One ½-in.-dia. button

One 4-in.-square crinoline
   (see Resources on p. 140)

½ yd. stable fusible interfacing

Thread to match

• Polyester topstitching thread

• Polyester sewing thread

Two sew-on rings

THE IDEA FOR THIS KNOT of ribbon is borrowed from vintage ornamentation worn on a hat or as a French badge or insignia. The outer folds are 1½-in.-wide grosgrain ribbon and the inner folds are 1-in.-wide grosgrain. An iridescent glass button adorns the center of a gathered ribbon rosette. The 4½-in.-dia. cocard is sewn to a 16-in.-long tieback constructed from two widths of matching grosgrain ribbon. The materials listed are for one tieback.

Step 1

preparation

① From the 1½-in.-wide grosgrain ribbon, cut fourteen 4-in. pieces and cut one 17-in. piece or the appropriate length for your tieback.

② From the 1-in.-wide grosgrain ribbon, cut fourteen 3-in. pieces and cut one 17-in. piece or the appropriate length for your tieback.

③ From the 1½-in.-wide silk ribbon, cut one 6-in. piece.

④ Cut one piece of fusible interfacing the length of your tieback and slightly narrower than the total width.

construction

① Fold each 1½-in. ribbon piece in half with wrong sides together. Using a knotted length of topstitching thread, insert a needle into one corner of each folded section about ⅛ in. inside the top raw edges and right finished edge. Allow about 1 in. of thread between the first knot and the last strung piece, then knot the thread after the last piece.

Step 2

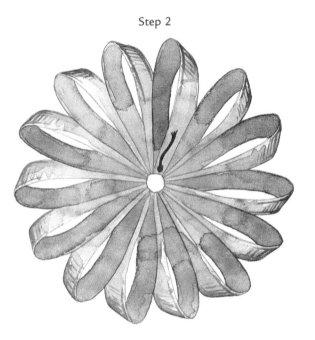

✳ The best grosgrain ribbon is made of 100% rayon. It is softer, easier to work with, and has a quality look.

②　Form a complete circle and join the ribbon folds with two stitches. Trim the thread.

③　Next, place the ribbon group on the crinoline. Flatten the ribbon circle, and place each folded petal equidistant from one another. Pin the raw edges to the crinoline and hand-tack each petal in place. Trim the crinoline so that it is well behind the cocard.

Step 3

④　Using the 1-in. grosgrain ribbon, repeat steps 1 and 2. Pin this second ribbon group on top of the first and hand-tack in place.

⑤　To join the cut ends of the silk piece, hand- or machine-sew a small seam. Fold the ribbon in half lengthwise to form a ring.

⑥　Using polyester thread, hand-sew a running stitch along the length of the raw edges of the folded silk ribbon through both layers. Gather the ribbon along the thread length until it forms a rosette, then knot the thread end to secure.

Step 5

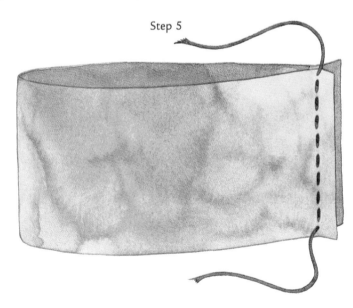

Step 6

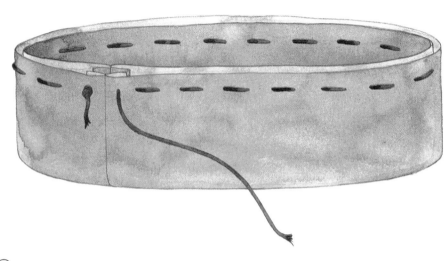

7 Hand-tack the rosette to the center of the cocard, then sew a button in the center of the rosette to cover the raw edges.

8 On a pressing surface, place the two strips of tieback grosgrain ribbon next to one another with wrong sides up. Place the strip of fusible interfacing on top of the two ribbons with the fusible side down. Using a press cloth, fuse the interfacing to the ribbons.

Step 7

9 Fold the ends of the tieback to the wrong side and stitch to finish. Attach a small ring to each end, then place the tieback on the drapery and pin the cocard in place. Remove the tieback and hand-tack the cocard to the tieback.

Step 8

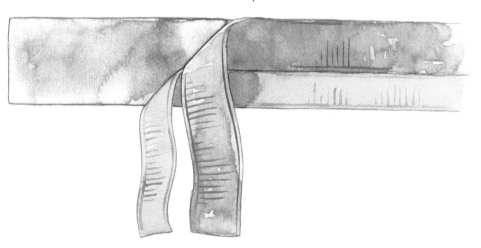

scallop flange pillow

FINISHED SIZE: 21 IN. BY 21 IN.

« **materials**

1½ yd. fabric

2¾ yd. decorative cord with
   a flange

One 16-in.-square pillow form

Two buttons at least 1¼ in. dia.

Thread to match

THE DESIGN OF THE FABRIC inspired the look of this pillow. This silk taffeta fabric has wide, even, mirror-image stripes and a fairly large striped section of a small gingham check. The size of the stripes dictates how the pieces are cut and how they intersect. The striped triangles are cut and matched to form an interlocking center. The slightly scalloped flange has a black and white silky cord inserted in the seam. The flange appears to be sewn onto the edge of the pillow, but it actually extends into the body, and a stitching line defines the size of the pillow. Buttons decorate the center of each side. The center square of triangles measures 12 in. Although the actual pillow is 16 in. square, it measures 21 in. by 21 in. including the flange.

Step 1

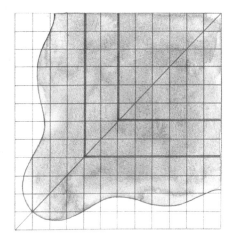

1 square = 1 inch

preparation

1 On a large piece of pattern paper, draw the pillow design. Work with the design of your fabric to determine the size of the center triangles. Draw one-half of one scalloped edge, then fold the paper in half and trace the pencil line to mark the other half of the scallops. Fold the paper three more times to trace all four scalloped edges.

2 Cut out one triangle pattern piece and one scallop/extension pattern.

3 Next, lay the paper triangle on the striped fabric so that the stripes are

✱ Extra fabric is required to work out special design details when using a stripe or plaid.

perpendicular to the long edge of the triangle. Mark where the stripes intersect the angled sides of the paper triangle, then cut out this triangle, adding ½-in. seam allowances.

④ Repeat to cut seven more triangles, using the markings on the paper to lay the pattern in the same place on the stripes for each piece.

⑤ Cut out eight scallop/extension pieces, adding ½-in. seam allowances.

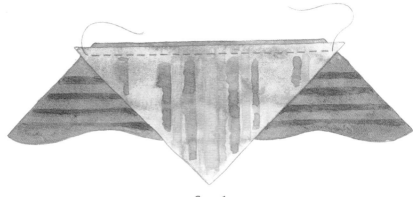

Step 1

construction

① With right sides together, sew one scallop/extension to the long edge of one triangle and press the seam open. Repeat for six more sections.

② For the eighth triangle section, sew about 1 in. of each seam end only, leaving an opening in the center.

③ With right sides together, sew one angled edge of two triangles, then press the seam open. Repeat three more times.

④ To make one complete pillow top, sew the long edges of two large triangles with right sides together. Press the seam open. Repeat to make one more complete top.

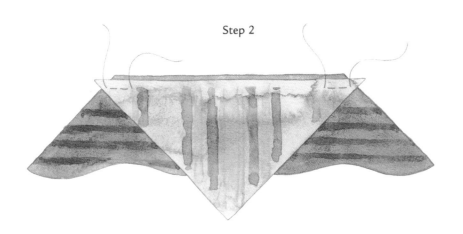

Step 2

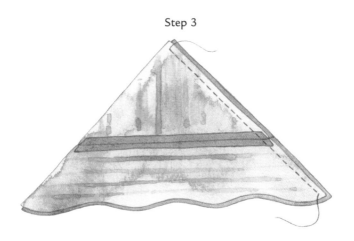

Step 3

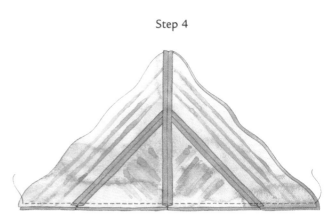

Step 4

Step 6

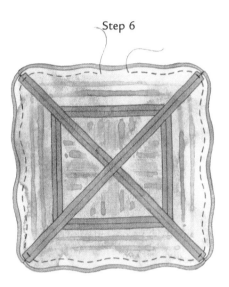

⑤ With the edge of the flange aligned with the outer edge of the scallops, sew the trim to each pillow top. Finish the ends neatly (see the sidebar below).

⑥ With right sides together, sew the pillow tops around all sides of the scallops. Turn to the outside and finger-press the edges.

⑦ Stitch both layers of the pillow together at the pillow edge line.

⑧ Sew a button at the center of each side of the pillow.

⑨ Finally, insert the pillow form through the opening and slipstitch.

Step 7

finishing trim neatly

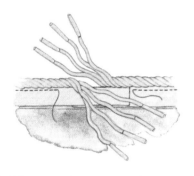

1. When starting to sew trim to an edge, leave about 2 in. of extra trim. When you are coming back around and are about to end the trim, stop sewing about 2 in. from the previous stitching and leave about 2 in. of extra trim.

2. Cut the flange away from the cord on the extra trim. Untwist the strands of the cord, and tape the ends to prevent raveling. Overlap and tape the excess flange in the seam allowance of the pillow.

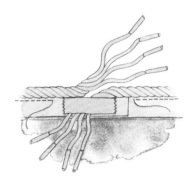

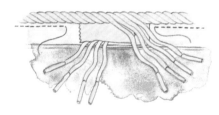

3. Twist and reweave the strands to mimic the original pattern of the cord.

4. Tape in place and stitch down.

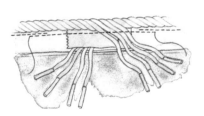

fragments and fringe pillow

« materials

Fabrics

- 1/2 yd. tapestry
- 2/3 yd. chenille damask
- 1/4 yd. organza
- 1/4 yd. dupioni

2 1/2 yd. fringe

2 yd. braid

Four rosettes

Thread to match

One 22-in. square pillow form

★ Experiment with different colors of underlining behind the organza to see how the color "reads." You can completely change the tone of a sheer fabric by underlining it.

★ The side organza and damask bands need to be at least 4 in. wide. If any narrower than that, they begin to disappear when the form is inserted.

THIS DOWN-FILLED PILLOW combines a group of luxurious fabrics in a windowpane design. The central fabric is a rich tapestry floral fabric. It is surrounded by pieces of velvet damask and underlined silk organza. Multicolored braid covers the surface seams, matching rosettes are applied to each seam connection, and matching looped fringe frames the edge.

preparation

1. Choose an interesting motif on the tapestry fabric and mark the center. Cut one 14-in. square.

2. Cut two pieces of chenille damask 22 in. by 5 in.

3. Cut two pieces of organza and two pieces of lining 14 in. by 5 in. With the wrong side of the organza facing the right side of the lining, baste the pieces together around all edges.

4. For the pillow back, cut one piece of damask 22 in. by 22 in.

5. From the braid, cut two pieces 22 in. long and two pieces 14 in. long.

6. Cut one piece of fringe 90 in. long.

★ When combining fabrics for pieced pillow tops, remember to consider "visual weight." All of the fabrics should appear to be of similar thickness and weight, even though they may not be. Stand back from them a few feet, put a hand over one eye or squint, and see if they seem similar.

Step 1

construction

① With right sides together, sew the underlined organza bands to both sides of the tapestry center. Press the seams toward the outside.

② Sew the damask bands to the top and bottom of the central tapestry with right sides together (see the illustration on p. 54). Press the seams toward the outside.

Step 2

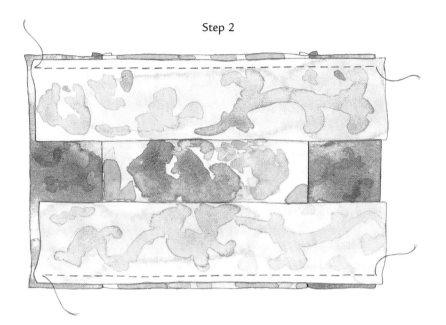

Step 3

Step 5

③ Next, center the shorter pieces of braid over the side seams. Depending on the size of the braid, either sew down the middle or on each side.

④ Center the longer pieces of braid over the top and bottom seams, then stitch to the pillow top.

⑤ Center the rosettes over the seam connections, and hand-sew to secure.

⑥ Overlapping the flange about 1 in., sew the fringe to the outer edges of the pillow top.

⑦ Lay the pillow top over the back and recut to fit. With right sides together, sew the top to the back, leaving an opening along one side. Turn to the outside.

⑧ Insert the pillow form and slipstitch the opening.

Step 7

lampshade slipcover

T HE PRIMARY FABRIC used in this lampshade cover is a medium-sheer cotton lace trimmed with a matching silk taffeta pleated ruffle and casing. A ½-in. elastic fed through an oversized casing simulates ruching and holds the skirt onto the shade. The taffeta ruffle is pleated and trimmed with delicate ribbon braid.

FINISHED SIZE: VARIABLE

« materials

- Lace
- Silk taffeta
- Ribbon trim
- ½-in.-wide elastic
- Thread to match

preparation

1 Measure your shade's circumference around the top and its height.

2 For the lace cover, cut a rectangle as follows: Multiply the shade's circumference by 1.5 to determine the width. To the height of the shade, add ½ in. for the bottom seam allowance and 1½ in. for the top heading.

3 For the taffeta casing, cut one piece of fabric about 1½ in. longer than the width of the rectangle by 1⅝ in. wide.

4 For the taffeta ruffle, cut one piece of fabric the width of the rectangle times 2 by 3½ in. wide.

⑤ Cut one piece of trim the width of the rectangle.

⑥ Cut one piece of elastic 2 in. smaller than the circumference of the shade top.

construction

① Using a French seam, sew the short ends of the rectangle together.

② Fold the ruffle strip in half lengthwise with wrong sides together. Do not press. Make a ½-in. pleat about every 1 in., then baste along the top seam allowance to hold the pleats in place.

Step 1

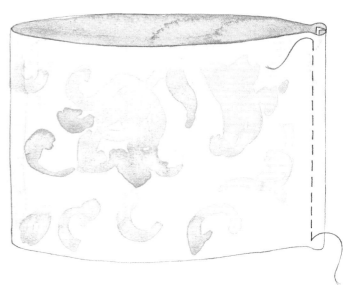

Step 2

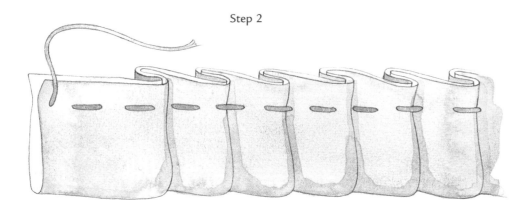

③ With right sides together, pin the ruffle to the bottom edge of the cover. Mark where the ruffle ends meet and sew a French seam, then repin the ruffle and sew to the cover. Stitch the raw edges together and press the seam toward the cover.

Step 3

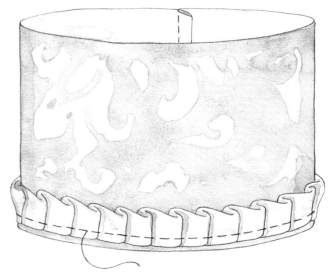

Step 4

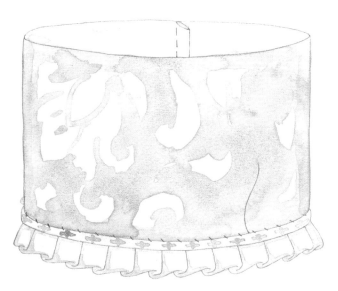

Step 5

4 Hand-tack the ribbon trim over the seam, and join neatly at the ends.

5 To form the heading, press ³⁄₄ in. to the right side of the top of the cover.

6 Press ¹⁄₄ in. to the wrong side of each long edge of the casing strip, and press one end under about ¹⁄₂ in. Place one long edge along the raw edge of the pressed heading, lapping the finished edge over the unfinished end. Edgestitch along the edge of the casing through all layers, then edgestitch the other edge of the casing.

7 Insert the elastic through the casing and secure at the ends. Place the slipcover over the shade and adjust the ruched casing evenly.

Step 6

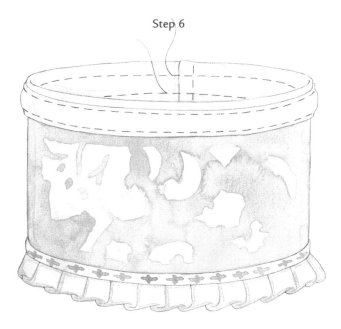

silk and lace throw

FINISHED SIZE: *42 IN. BY 73 IN.*

‹‹ m a t e r i a l s

3 yd. heavy silk charmeuse

1¼ yd. lace, at least 36 in. wide
   with scalloped edge borders on
   both sides

1 yd. silk crepe de Chine

2½ yd. fringe/lace trim
   with pearl accents

Contrasting basting thread

THIS LUSCIOUS double-sided throw is constructed like a large pillowcase—open on one end. The primary fabric is a heavy silk charmeuse trimmed at one end with a scallop-edged heavy lace. Flat piping in silk crepe de Chine trims both side seams and one end seam, and a delicate fringed trim with pearl accents adorns the seam between the silk and lace. Individual floral motifs from the lace have been cut out and used as corner appliqués, and three pearls are sewn to the center of each motif. The throw measures 42 in. by 73 in., with the lace accounting for 19 in. of the length.

preparation

1 From the silk charmeuse, cut two pieces 43 in. by 55 in.

2 From the lace yardage, cut down the center of the width of the lace to make two pieces of fabric about 19 in. wide with a scalloped border on one edge only.

3 From the crepe de Chine, cut 1¼-in.-wide pieces of bias and join them together to make two 55-in. strips and one 43-in. strip.

Step 1

construction

1 Fold each crepe de Chine bias strip in half lengthwise with the wrong sides together and press. Matching all raw edges, baste the strips to one end and to each side of one piece of silk charmeuse along the seamline.

2 With right sides together, sew the silk charmeuse pieces together along the previous basting line. Turn to the outside and press.

Step 3

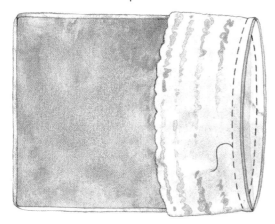

Step 5

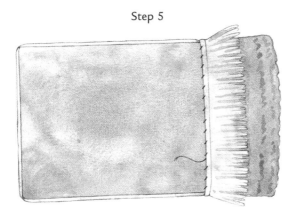

③ Using a lapped-seam technique (see the sidebar below), sew the lace together, creating a tube in size to match the open end of the charmeuse. With right sides together, sew the cut end of the lace to the raw edges of the charmeuse "pillowcase." Serge-finish the raw edges together, and press toward the charmeuse.

④ Cut four floral motifs out of the lace scraps, then hand-tack to both sides of the two upper corners of the charmeuse. Hand-sew pearl accents to the floral center.

⑤ Pin lace fringe over the lace/charmeuse seam, joining the ends neatly. Hand-tack in place.

sewing invisible lapped seams

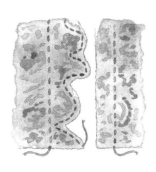

1. When preparing to cut a lace seam, thread-trace straight lines along each seamline of the pieces that are to be joined. On the overlapping piece, thread-trace the motif outline outside the seamline. Allow plenty of seam allowance for the underlap piece.

2. Overlap the seamlines along the thread-tracing lines, and baste the extended motifs to the adjoining piece.

3. Using small whipstitches by hand or using machine zigzag stitches in matching thread, appliqué the motif edge to the underlapped piece of lace.

4. With small, sharp trimming scissors, trim the "whiskers" on the top side and trim away the seam allowance close to the stitching on the underlapping side.

inverted pleat slipcover

THIS SIMPLE CHAIR-SEAT slipcover is constructed in an allover Chinoiserie patterned, glazed chintz fabric. The seat top is darted to create shape. Contrasting baby piped cording separates an apron, which supports an inverted pleat ruffle. Buttons and loops provide closures where the back and arms connect to the chair.

FINISHED SIZE: VARIABLE

« materials

Fabric

Contrasting fabric for
    piped cording

Muslin

Rattail cord or small cotton
    cable cord

Buttons

Thread to match

preparation

1 To make the pattern, start by cutting a square of muslin larger than the seat, then place it over the chair seat and pin in a few places.

Step 2

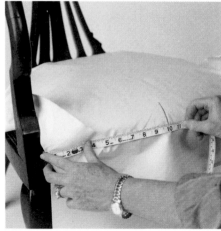

Step 3

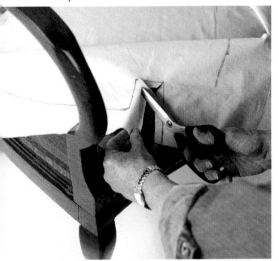

Step 4

② With a soft lead pencil, mark the center of the seat at the front and back. Wherever the fabric wants to ripple or pucker or the shapes need a curve, pin a dart.

③ Mark where the arm and back connect to the seat, and cut away the fabric around these as needed so that the muslin will lie flat and smooth.

④ Trace the outline of the chair onto the muslin. This is the place where there is typically a seam or a welt or where the upholstery dies into the wood frame.

⑤ Next, pin strips of muslin to the edge of the chair seat muslin on the marked line to determine the width of the apron and the placement of closure overlaps at the center back and sides. Closures are typically constructed at some point near the arms and back. Pin more than one apron band onto the seat cover, experimenting with the right closure and the amount of overlap needed for a smooth fit with no gapping. Reposition the band, if needed, so that it lies flat and vertical.

⑥ Mark the connection points on the apron sections and indicate button and loop locations.

⑦ To simulate the skirt, pin wider strips of muslin to the bottom of the apron, stopping and starting them in the same places as the apron sections. Mark the location of the center of the legs to determine the placement of the inverted pleats.

Step 5

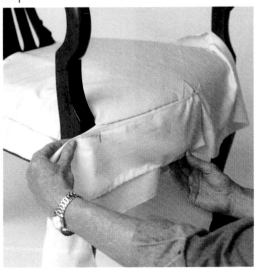

Step 6

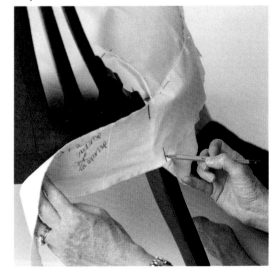

Step 7

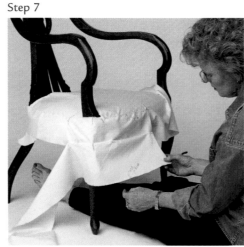

⑧ Standing back, study the proportions of the components of the slipcover to the height and scale of the chair, and make adjustments as needed.

⑨ Make any other notes on the muslin pieces that are important, such as hem allowances, depth of inverted pleats, and center lines.

⑩ Next, remove the muslin pieces from the chair, and add ½-in. seam allowances and 1-in. hem allowances to all pieces. Fold the chair seat in half along the center line, then cut through both layers following the pencil markings to create a mirror-image, full-sized pattern.

Step 10

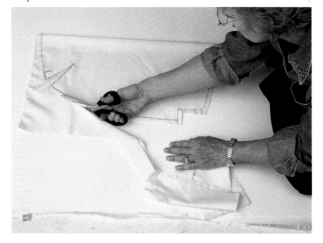

⑪ Using the muslin as your pattern, cut out the chair seat, the apron pieces, and the skirt pieces. Add allowances for the inverted pleats to the skirt pieces. The pleats should be at least 2 in. deep. If you need to piece the skirt sections, make the seams inside the inverted pleats.

⑫ Using the contrasting fabric, cut 1½-in.-wide strips of bias for the piped cording and 1-in.-wide strips for the loops.

construction

① With right sides together, stitch the darts in the chair seat.

② To make the cutout facings, cut squares of fabric about 2 in. larger than the cutouts for the legs and arms, then serge-finish or press under the outer edges. With right sides together, pin a square over each cutout on the chair seat. Stitch around the opening, pivoting at the corners. Clip to the corners and trim the seams, then press the facing to the wrong side.

Step 2

Step 3

Step 3 (detail)

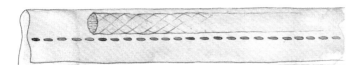

Step 5

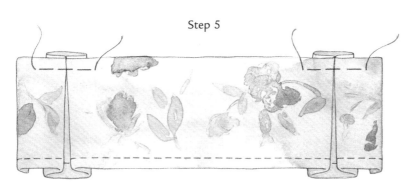

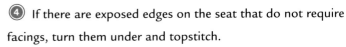

3 Make enough baby corded piping to go around both the top and bottom of each apron piece, then sew the piping to the edges. Pull the fabric covering away from the ends of the cord, and trim away enough cord to keep it out of each seam or hem allowance. Press the short ends of the aprons to the wrong side to finish.

4 If there are exposed edges on the seat that do not require facings, turn them under and topstitch.

5 Serge-finish the bottom edges of the skirt sections, and press the hems to the wrong side and topstitch. Fold the fabric to form inverted pleats where marked, and baste across the top of the pleat. Press the short ends of the skirt sections to the wrong side to finish.

6 With right sides together, stitch the skirt sections to the bottom edges of the apron. Topstitch the ends of the skirt and apron sections in one step.

7 Next, sew the top edge of the apron/skirt pieces to the outer edges of the chair seat with right sides together.

8 Finally, make button loops for the back and sides of the chair openings. Sew the raw ends of the loops to the underside of the band overlaps, and sew the buttons in the corresponding places on the apron underlaps.

Step 6

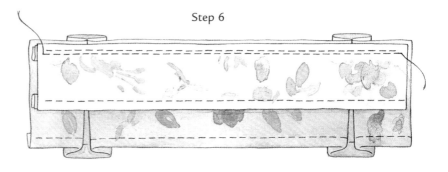

Step 7

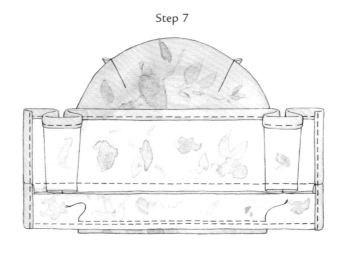

tuffet

A FOUR-LEGGED STOOL, found at a flea market, provides the base structure for this tuffet. The top is upholstered in a cotton tapestry fabric, the side band is upholstered in a silk plaid taffeta, and the bottom is finished with 7-in. bullion fringe. Decorative braided cord is loosely swagged around the tuffet and tied in four places with tassels and large buttons.

FINISHED SIZE: VARIABLE

« materials

One ottoman or stool

1 yd. tapestry fabric

½ yd. silk taffeta (allow additional
 fabric to match plaids)

2¼ yd. of 7-in. bullion fringe

4½ yd. twisted decorative cord
 without a flange

2¼ yd. twisted decorative cord
 with a flange

Four tassels

Four large buttons or other
 decorative ornaments

Two pieces of 3-in.-thick foam
 at least 30 in. square

½ yd. cotton batting

¾ yd. cambric dust cover
 (see Resources on p. 140)

2½ yd. cardboard tack strip
 (see Resources on p. 140)

1 yd. polyester batting

1 yd. muslin

Heavyweight upholstery thread

preparation

① To cut the tapestry fabric, determine where the seat top will begin and end. Measure the diameter of the seat top, and cut a square about 4 in. wider than that measurement.

② To cut the silk taffeta, measure from the floor to the seat-top line. Subtract the height of the bullion trim to determine the height of the taffeta band, then add seam allowances to this

* The yardages given for this tuffet are based on using a stool that is 22 in. in diameter and 19 in. high. Adjust, if needed.

* The best tool to cut foam is an electric kitchen knife.

measurement. Cut two widths of fabric to this height. Sew two short ends together to make one long band, then measure the circumference of the stool and cut the strip to this length plus seam allowances.

③ To cut the bullion fringe trim, cut the fringe the same length as the circumference of the stool plus about 2 in. for finishing.

④ Since the decorative cord without a flange will swag around the tuffet, experiment with swagging the cord four times around the stool, then double this measurement. Cut to length, allowing several extra inches of cord.

* Cording can normally be ordered with or without a flange. If it is available only with a flange, the tape extension can be removed by careful cutting.

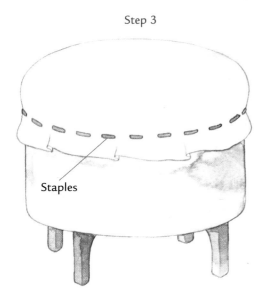

Step 3

Staples

⑤ Since the decorative cord with a flange is used once around the stool, cut it the same length as the circumference of the stool plus a few inches.

⑥ For the foam, cut one circle 2 in. smaller than the diameter of the stool top. Cut another circle 6 in. larger than the diameter of the stool top.

⑦ Cut enough cotton batting to cover the side band area.

⑧ Next, cut one circle of the cambric dust cover the size of the bottom of the stool plus a seam allowance.

⑨ Cut one piece of the cardboard tack strip equal to the circumference of the stool at the top of the band.

construction

① Place the smallest foam piece on top of the seat, then place the larger piece of foam on top of the smaller.

② both pieces of foam with one layer of polyester batting. Wrap the edges, staple around the bottom of the seat top, and cut off the excess batting.

③ Next, cover the batting with one piece of muslin to prevent the batting from sticking through the upholstery fabric. Start by stapling in four places around the seat, then staple in between the first staples, pulling taut as you go. Trim the excess muslin.

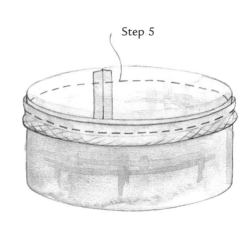

Step 5

Step 6

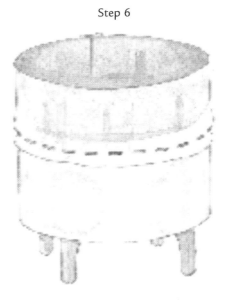

④ Place the tapestry on top of the muslin, and staple the tapestry in place, repeating the process for attaching the muslin. Cut away the excess.

⑤ Sew the ends of the band together to fit the circumference of the stool exactly. Matching the flange edge of the trim to the top raw edge of the band, sew the cord to the band. Glue the ends of the cord to prevent raveling.

⑥ Slipping the band onto the stool from the bottom, position the cord along the staple line and pull the band completely up so that it is upside down and the cord is on the inside. Staple along the seam allowance of the band and cord.

Step 7

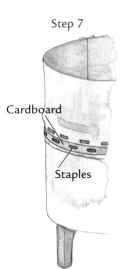

Cardboard

Staples

⑦ Staple the cardboard tack strip over the seam allowance of the band and cord.

⑧ Next, staple a thin layer of cotton batting over the area that the band will cover. Pull the band down to cover the batting, then staple in place along the bottom.

⑨ On the circle of cambric, fold the seam allowance under and staple to the bottom of the stool.

Step 8

⑩ Glue the bullion fringe in place, covering the staples of the bottom of the band. Reweave the ends of the gimp portion of the fringe and glue to prevent raveling.

⑪ Finally, swag the plain cord twice in four places around the stool, and staple or glue the ends in place. Tie, staple, or glue the tassels at each swag attachment. Using a curved needle, sew large buttons or other ornaments over the tassel ends.

Step 10

Step 11

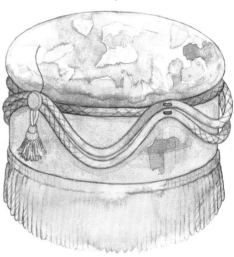

>> 67

octagonal table topper

FINISHED SIZE: VARIABLE

« materials

Fabrics (45 in. wide)

- ¼ yd. each of five colors
- ⅓ yd. each of six colors
- ¾ yd. of one color

1⅔ yd. lining (45 in. wide)

1⅔ yd. muslin or large
   drawing paper

Template material

Thread to match

THIS OCTAGON-SHAPED TABLE COVER has pieced geometric shapes in 12 colors of silk dupioni. Each band around the central octagon consists of shades from a color group. The cover is lined in China silk and edged with a 1-in.- wide, dark-toned silk dupioni. The table measures 29 in. wide from edge to edge and 29 in. high, while its cover is 49 in. from edge to edge (29 in. wide plus two 10-in. drops).

preparation

① Measure the circumference or width of the table top and record the number. Add the drop twice (the drop should be about one-third the height of the table).

② Draw a scaled drawing of the complete cover, including the pieced shapes. Using colored pencils, color in the fabric selections for each row. Assign an identifying letter for each different shape and a number for each row.

③ On a large piece of muslin or drawing paper, draw a full-scale design, then use the full-size drawing as a pattern for making individual templates for the pieced shapes. Add ¼-in. seam allowances to all sides of the templates.

④ Using the templates on p. 70, cut out all the pieces. Start by cutting out eight 1½-in.-wide strips for the outer bands.

Step 2

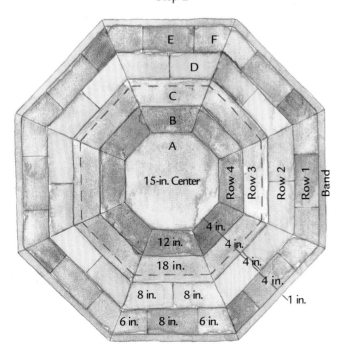

Step 4

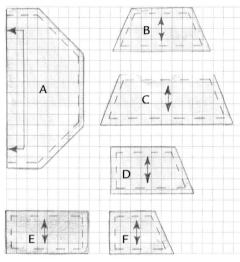

1 square = 1 inch

Step 1

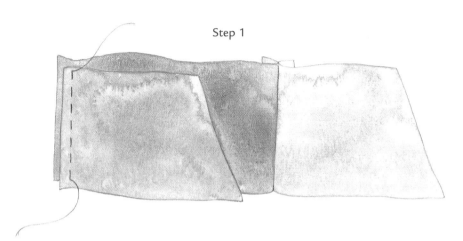

⑤ If the finished width of the cover is wider than the fabric width, sew widths of lining together before cutting the finished shape. Cut the final shape after the pieced top has been completed.

construction

① With right sides together, sew the sections of each row in each wedge together. Press seams open.

② Sew one short edge of one band to the long edge of row one with right sides together, then press the seam open.

③ With right sides together, sew the short edge of row one to the long edge of row two. Press the seam open.

④ Sew the short edge of row two to the short edge of row three, then press the seam open.

⑤ Sew the short edge of row three to the long edge of row four. Press the seam open.

Step 2

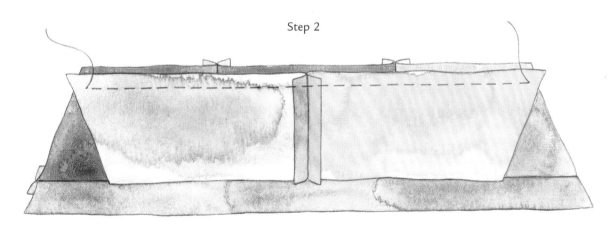

Step 7

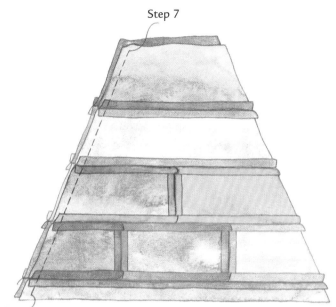

⑥ Complete eight wedges by sewing all rows together.

⑦ With right sides together, sew one side of a wedge to the side of another wedge, maintaining the order of the original scaled and colored drawing. Sew to within ¼ in. of the inner edge, then press the seam open. Repeat for all of the wedges until a full circle is complete.

⑧ Sew one edge of the center at a time to the short edges of the wedges, stopping and starting the stitching at each wedge seam. Press the seams toward the center.

⑨ Lay the right side of the pieced top on the right side of the lining, then cut the lining to fit the pieced top. Sew around all edges, leaving an opening along one wedge. Turn to the outside and slipstitch the opening.

Step 8

Step 9

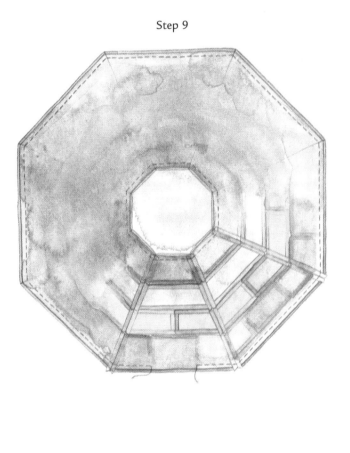

crinkled table skirt

FINISHED SIZE: *VARIABLE*

« materials

- Crinkled silk metallic organza
- Silk metallic organza
- Muslin
- Thread to match
- Gimp cord

✻ If you can't find crinkled organza, use China silk as a substitute. To crinkle China silk, wet and twist it until it forms a fairly tight ball. Hold the ball in place with string or thread, slip it into a piece of hosiery, and allow it to dry naturally or in a clothes dryer. The result is a randomly crinkled, lustrous piece of fabric.

THIS COMPANION UNDERSKIRT to the pieced table topper (see pp. 68–71) is a separate petticoat attached to a muslin center. The decorative skirt is made of crinkled silk metallic organza and underlined with noncrinkled silk metallic organza. Both are cut into wedges and shirred onto an eight-sided center that is slightly smaller than the topper.

preparation

1 Measure the width and height of the table, then multiply the height times two and add this figure to the width to get the total diameter.

2 For the muslin center, measure the finished diameter of the table topper. Subtract 4 in. and cut a muslin center in an octagonal shape.

3 For the petticoat wedges, subtract the diameter of the center from the total diameter to determine the minimum height of the petticoat wedges. Add at least 5 in. to this length to allow the wedges to "puddle." Each wedge should be at least 1½ times as wide as each side of the octagon center. The plain underlining can be cut to fit the octagon sides exactly.

Step 3

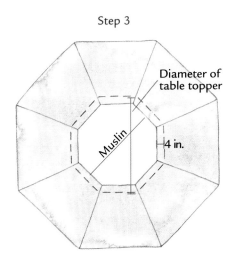

Diameter of table topper

Muslin

4 in.

construction

1 With right sides together, sew the side of one crinkled wedge to the side of another and press the seam open. Stitch all the wedges together to form a complete tube.

2 Sew the sides of the lining wedges with right sides together to form a complete tube.

3 Using a narrow baby hem, hem the bottom of the crinkled skirt and the lining.

Step 3

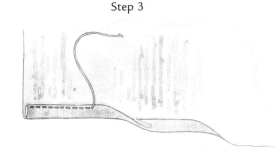

5 With right sides together, sew the skirt to the outer edges of the muslin center. Press the seams to the center.

Step 2

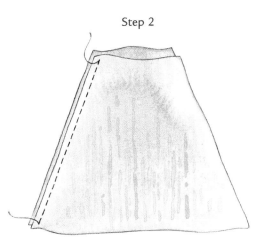

4 At the top of the tube, zigzag-stitch over gimp cord. Anchor one end of the cord with a pin, then pull the cord to gather the crinkled tube along the top. Baste the outer skirt to the lining at the top.

Step 4

CHAPTER 3

Asian dining room

T HE AMERICAN FASCINATION with Asian arts and culture has permeated our fashion sense for centuries. In such things as our textiles, design motifs, color, and lifestyle, no other influence has been as recognizable as that from the Far East. As the kimono import market dwindles and fewer original kimonos are available, we are using smaller bits of less-important kimono textiles to enhance and accessorize our clothing and interiors and to preserve these great finds.

The pagoda form is as usable today as a design motif as it was of use as an architectural element early on. Even if you don't know the meaning of the figures, the Chinese alphabet characters are beautiful graphic symbols. Frog closures remind us that our newer inventions, such as the zipper, are clumsy and unnecessary. And who wants to drink tea from an ordinary vessel, especially if it is cold?

The dining room setting incorporates many of the influences from the Orient into a fresh, modern setting.

Inspired by the rattan frames on the dining chairs, I found it natural to incorporate Asian influences and details into this dining room setting. Using vintage kimono fabrics and fabrics woven with Chinese alphabet characters, a table runner and place mats were added to this contemporary parson's table. Uniquely shaped tea cozies for Japanese teapots and embroidered napkins wrapped with semi-precious stone, jade, and Chinese coin napkin rings accessorize the table. Even the chairs have sheer slipcovers tied with handmade frog closures to add an Asian touch.

Transitional fabrics in matelassé double weaves, muted damasks, and small jacquard patterns in exquisite golden hues, muted greens, and putty provide a peaceful, monochromatic palette. It is useful to start with an allover print fabric, such as a floral, in colors that are pleasing and then pull in other fabrics from the range of color possibilities in the print.

Slipcovers made in *shoji*-like sheer panels, attached to interesting bamboo-framed chairs with whimsical petal frogs, insulated tea cozies to cover petite Japanese tea pots, an ensemble of place mats, and a table runner trimmed with a potpourri of pieced kimono fabrics and accessorized with embroidered napkins and jewel-like napkin rings set the stage for an incredible dining experience. Beautiful fabrics with unique trimmings and details make these easy projects sing.

The same concepts used in the Asian dining room still work when the furniture is more streamlined and contemporary. Simple fabric panels with ties change the look of an all-upholstered chair. Mixed textures and prints create borders for the table runner and place mats and coordinate with the tea cozies.

kimono border table runner

« materials

Fabrics
- Ground fabric
- Lining fabric
- 15 to 20 coordinated kimono fabrics (see Resources on p. 140)

Thread to match

THE GROUND FABRIC used in this table runner is an upholstery-weight matelassé. Ladderlike strips of kimono fabric separate three center sections. The runner is bordered by pieced sections of kimono fabrics, and the entire runner is lined with the same matelassé as the ground. It measures 16 in. by 131 in.

preparation

1 Measure the length and width of the table.

2 To determine the table runner length, add the overhang on both ends plus $\frac{1}{2}$-in. seam allowances to the length of the table. An overhang of about 8 in. is fairly standard.

3 For the width of the table runner, use about one-third the table width plus $\frac{1}{2}$-in. seam allowances as the dimension.

4 Allowing for 2-in. borders and $\frac{1}{2}$-in. ladder separations, cut three sections of ground fabric, adding $\frac{1}{2}$-in. seam allowances.

5 Cut one piece of lining the overall size, including borders, ladders, and $\frac{1}{2}$-in. seam allowances.

6 Next, cut enough 3-in. squares with $\frac{1}{4}$-in. seam allowances of several kimono fabrics to border four sides of the runner.

7 Cut two $1\frac{1}{2}$-in.-wide strips with $\frac{1}{2}$-in. seam allowances of kimono fabric for the ladders.

Step 1

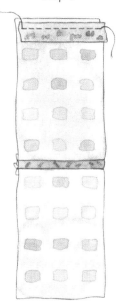

construction

1 With right sides together, sew one ground section to one long edge of a ladder, and press the seam open. Continue in this manner until the three ground sections are sewn to two ladders.

2 With right sides together, sew one 3-in. square of kimono fabric to another square, and press the seam open. Continue piecing two lengths to match each end of the runner.

Step 2

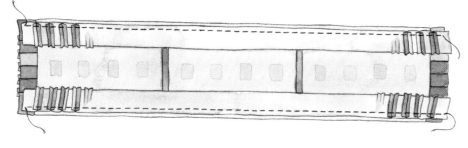

3 Sew the strips to each end of the runner with right sides together. Press the seam open.

4 Repeating step two, piece two strips of kimono fabrics the length of each side. With right sides together, sew the strips to each side, pressing the seams open.

5 Place the right side of the lining on top of the pieced runner, then stitch around all four sides, leaving an opening. Trim the corners, turn the runner to the outside, slipstitch the opening, and press.

Step 3

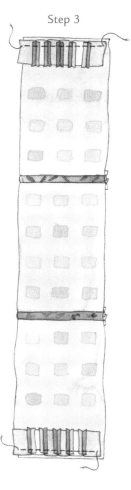

Step 4

pagoda place mats

THE FABRIC USED in the central portion of this place mat is a tone-on-tone damask with an Asian alphabet design. The ends are pieced sections of kimono fabrics emulating pagoda rooftop shapes. The place mat is lined with the same fabric as the center. It measures 13 in. by 20½ in. from tip to tip.

FINISHED SIZE: 13 IN. BY 20½ IN.

<< **materials**

Fabrics for one place mat

- ½ yd. damask fabric
- ¼-yd. pieces of six kimono fabrics (see Resources on p. 140)

Thread to match

preparation

1 Using the scaled design shown below, make two tagboard shapes for the pieced sides. Include ¼-in. seam allowances.

Step 1

1 square = 1 inch

2 Using different kimono fabrics, cut four corners and two centers.

3 Cut one 11¾-in. by 12¾-in. piece of damask fabric.

4 Cut one rectangle of damask fabric no smaller than 15 in. by 22 in.

Step 1

construction

1 With right sides together, sew the longest straight edge of one kimono fabric corner to the corresponding side edge of a center piece. Press the seam open. Repeat to sew all the corners to the centers.

2 With right sides together, stitch the long straight edge of a pieced end to the longer side of the damask piece. Press the seam open, then repeat to attach the other pieced end.

Step 2

3 Place the place mat top on the damask rectangle with wrong sides together. Recut the rectangle to the exact shape and size of the top.

4 With right sides together, sew the place mat top to the lining around all four sides, leaving an opening. Trim the corners and turn to the outside, then slipstitch the opening and press.

Step 4

monogram napkin

THIS MEDIUM-WEIGHT LINEN NAPKIN is finished with a basic serger rolled hem. One corner of the napkin is embellished with a machine-embroidered Chinese character. The napkin measures 18 in. square.

FINISHED SIZE: 18 IN. BY 18 IN.

« materials

Medium-weight 100% linen

Rayon decorative thread one or two
    shades lighter than the fabric

Embroidery card with Chinese
    characters for your embroidery
    machine

Stabilizer

preparation

1 Cut squares of linen 4 in. to 6 in. larger than the finished size of the napkin.

* Rather than threading the serger tail back and under the previous stitching, use the thread tail as a means to hang beads and other baubles.

construction

1 Select the area to be mono-grammed, and place stabilizer on the wrong side. Following the instructions for your machine, embroider one character in the corner of each napkin using the rayon decorative thread. Remove the stabilizer.

2 Trim each napkin to be ¼ in. larger than the finished size.

Step 1

Step 3

3 Set your serger to a two- or three-thread rolled-hem stitch formation. Starting at one corner, hem all four sides of the napkin. Thread the chain tail onto a hand-sewing needle, then slip the needle under a few stitches of the hem and trim the thread.

beaded napkin ring

THESE EARRING-LIKE napkin rings are constructed using classic jewelry-making techniques. Beads in fluorite, quartz crystal, and garnet clusters are suspended from jade discs or antique reproduction coins. Velvet ribbons, slipped through silver double jump rings, tie around the napkins. The length of the beaded ornament is 3 in.

FINISHED SIZE: 3 IN. LONG

« materials

One silver decorative head pin

One fluorite bead
   (see Resources on p. 140)

One quartz crystal bead

One garnet or pearl cluster bead

One patina brass jump ring

One jade disc or antique
   reproduction coin

One sterling-silver toggle

One set silver double jump rings

⅓ yd. of ½-in.-wide velvet ribbon

Step 1

construction

1 Thread the decorative head pin through the fluorite bead, quartz crystal bead, and either the garnet or pearl cluster bead. The order of the beads can vary.

2 Using needle-nose pliers, wrap the end of the decorative head pin around the patina brass jump ring, and cut off the excess pin length.

3 Spread the ends of the patina brass jump ring apart sideways using flat-nose pliers, and slip the ring onto a jade disc or antique reproduction coin. Close the ring opening.

Step 2

Step 3

Step 4

4 Holding the silver toggle so that the shank is through the hole of the jade disc, feed the set of double jump rings through the shank. File any rough edges.

5 Slip velvet ribbon through the double jump rings, cutting the ribbon long enough to tie around a folded napkin.

shoji *slipcover*

THESE SIMPLE, SHEER SLIPCOVERS are straight panels of linen gauze that extend from the seat back, over the chair back, and hang to the floor. Topstitched wide hems and mitered corners finish the edges. Soutache-braid frogs with kimono fabric florettes tie the slipcover to each chair.

FINISHED SIZE: VARIABLE

« materials

Fabrics for one slipcover

- 1³/₄ yd. gauze fabric
- ¹/₈ yd. each of four kimono fabrics (see Resources on p. 140)

2 yd. soutache braid

Thread to match the fabric and the soutache braid

Polyester thread

preparation

❶ To determine the length of the slipcover, place a tape measure at the back of the chair seat and measure from that point up and over the chair back, ending the tape at the floor. Add 4 in. to this measurement.

❷ To determine the width, measure the width of the chair back between the side supports, and add 4 in. to this measurement.

3 Using the above measurements, cut one piece of gauze fabric.

4 Cut four pieces of kimono fabrics each 3 in. by 7 in.

5 Next, cut eight pieces of soutache braid each 8 in.

6 Cut a piece of tagboard 1 in. by 12 in.

construction

1 Place the tagboard strip 1 in. from one raw edge of the gauze panel. Bring the fabric up and over the bottom edge of the tagboard, matching the top edge, and press. Repeat to bring the folded edge to the top of the tagboard and press. Press the hems in place on all four sides of the panel.

Step 1

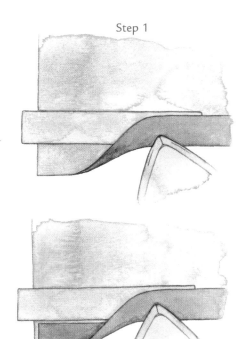

Step 2

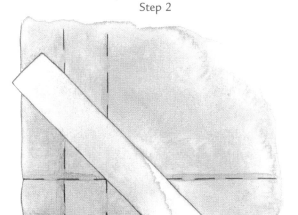

2 Unfold the hems at the corners, then place the tagboard diagonally across the corner at the intersection of the inner foldlines. Press the fabric over the tagboard.

3 With right sides together, match the raw edges and the diagonal creaseline to form a diagonal fold. Stitch from the fold to the first foldline and backstitch, then trim the excess fabric. Press the seam open over a point presser, turn to the outside, and press. Repeat at all four corners.

4 Topstitch around the entire panel next to the inner fold.

Step 3

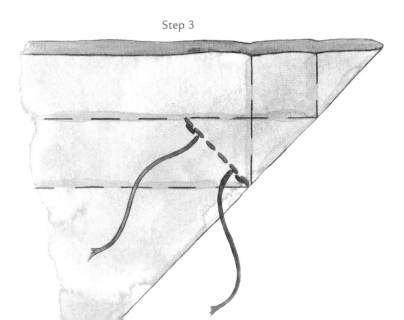

5 Placing the panel on the chair, mark the placement for the frog closures.

6 With right sides together, sew the short ends of each kimono piece together, then press the seam open.

7 With wrong sides together, fold the kimono pieces together lengthwise. Do not press. With a knotted polyester thread, stitch a running stitch around the raw edges of the kimono piece. Pull the thread to gather into a bell shape and knot to hold, leaving the thread tail attached.

Step 7

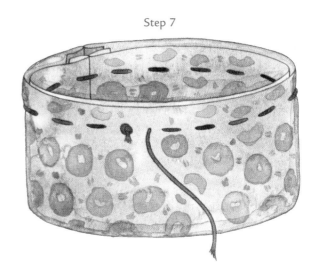

8 Fold each of four pieces of soutache braid in half to form a loop. Insert the cut ends into the opening of the gathered kimono flower and knot. Wrap the thread tail tightly around the gathered center and knot to secure, then pull the kimono flower over the gathered center to hide it. Clip the soutache ends close to the knot.

Step 8

9 Fold each of the remaining pieces of soutache to form a continuous loop, ends overlapping in the center. Drop the feed dogs on your sewing machine, and set the stitch to a wide zigzag. Place the loop under the presser foot and bar-tack in two places, leaving a large enough opening at one end to allow the flower to slip through. Trim the ends.

10 Hand-tack the frogs to the edges of the panel.

Step 9

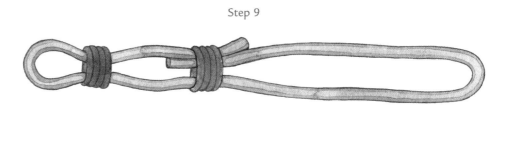

Japanese tea cozies

« materials

Fabrics for one tea cozy

- 1/4 yd. to 1/3 yd. each of four fabrics
- 1/4 yd. to 1/3 yd. thinsulate or cotton flannel (see Resources on p. 140)
- 1/4 yd. to 1/3 yd. silk for lining

Trim, buttons, or other embellishments

Thread to match

THESE CHARMING TEA COZIES are made from small remnants of silk dupioni, metallic glazed cottons, and matelassé silks. Silver rickrack, covered and stuffed balls, vintage buttons, and other baubles trim the edges and adorn the top. Each is underlined and insulated and lined with a contrasting silk fabric.

preparation

1 Copy the scaled illustrations shown below, which represent the shapes used in the sample cozies, or use them as starting points for your own designs. Start by making a paper pattern, taping the sections together, to test for size on your teapot.

2 Cut out each side in a different fabric, adding 1/4-in. seam allowances.

3 Cut out the same shape four times both in lining fabric and in Thinsulate or flannel.

Step 1

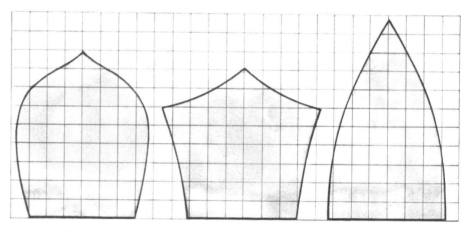

1 square = 1 inch

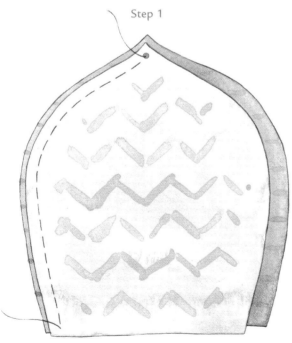

Step 1

construction

1 With right sides together, sew one side of one outer piece to another side, start the stitching where the two ¼-in. seam allowances join at the tip. Press the seams open over a tailor's board, the trim the bottom edges evenly. Repeat for all sides.

2 Repeat step 1 for the insulation layer and for the lining.

3 Next, place the layers in the following order, aligning the bottom edges: the right side of the lining to the wrong side of the outer fabric to the wrong side of the lining to the wrong side of the flannel.

Step 3

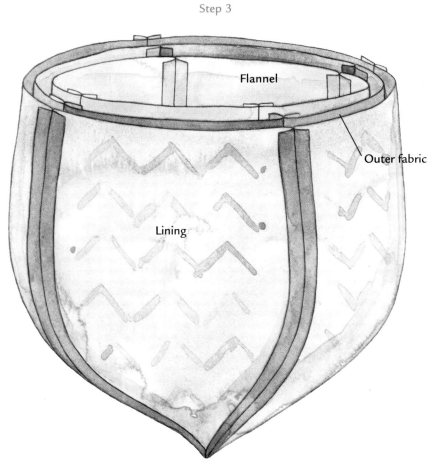

Flannel

Outer fabric

Lining

✳ If you are inserting piping or other trim, the trim should be sewn to one edge of each piece before joining the sections.

④ Sew the bottom edge, leaving about a 4-in. opening, then turn to the outside.

⑤ Reaching between the lining and the insulation, hand-sew the top embellishment in place, covering the hole where the seams come together.

⑥ Slipstitch the opening.

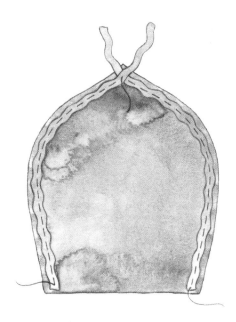

AMERICANA FAMILY ROOM

CHAPTER 4

Americana
family room

A SMALL, INTIMATE FAMILY ROOM is the coziest and safest place to be on earth. And it is even more so when it is filled with treasures from the past, treasures that are true to the American style and that have lived with generations before.

Some of our best things are handed down and some are acquired. Collecting and antiquing have become a serious hobby. The adventure of finding great furniture and collectibles is definitely a thrill. Some of our finds move right into a room without skipping a beat. Others may need a little help to make them right.

This quaint family room is really a very basic room when stripped down to its bones—wood floors, white walls, traditional fireplace, and mantel. Buy a simple leather sofa, add a few good pine pieces, adorn the walls with paintings and art, and you have the beginnings of a look. But your touch and the warmth is yet to come. Take the hard edge off of that leather sofa with a soft, fringed western-style pillow, and surround a

The Americana family room, with its classic deep colors and rich patterns and textures, is warm, comfortable, and cozy. Basic furniture is enhanced by adding a tapestry and lace mantel cover, a stenciled linen table cover, a soft afghan, a charming lace-trimmed basket liner, and unique fringed and tapestry pillows.

Blue, yellow, and white are popular colors in the country French style. Both wide and narrow stripes, a mini check and larger plaid, and two coordinating floral prints create a nice balance of patterns in varying scales. Smooth finishes and a hint of shine are perfect for a clean, bright room.

richly textured piece of tapestry with more soft suede.
Cover that not-so-near-perfect table with a slipcover,
laced at the corners with stenciled borders. Change the
simple fireplace by adding a dramatic tapestry and lace
mantel cover. And nothing adds warmth to a room like
a soft, jersey afghan for those cool, autumn evenings.
Think texture, rich colors, and soft materials, and you
have the perfect additions to your favorite room.

The character of this family room is
completely transformed when new
fabrics and finishes replace the heavier
Americana look. Less pattern, fewer
accessories, and the addition of white,
both in the table and fabrics, bring
sunshine into this very livable room.

autumn afghan

FINISHED SIZE: *52 in. by 67 in.*

« materials

100% washed wool jersey
- 2½ yd. of one color for the center of one side
- ¾ yd. each of six colors
- Small scraps of five to ten colors (may include some of the above colors)

2 yd. leopard faux fur

Fusible adhesive
(I like Fine Fuse by Solar-Kist Corporation; see Resources on p. 140)

Black thread

Thread to match

✳ If you wash your wool jersey and it doesn't shrink much, try cutting it into 2-yd. or 3-yd. pieces and washing it again. I have had to wash some wool jerseys as many as eight times to get the textured effect that I want.

THIS TWO-SIDED, COZY AFGHAN is made of washed wool jersey on one side and velvetlike leopard faux fur on the other. A solid-color central field of wool jersey is edged with a pieced wool jersey border. Colorful leaves, with three-dimensional veins and in different shapes and sizes, are appliquéd to the jersey side before assembling the two sides.

preparation

① Using the patterns shown on p. 105 as a guide, draw leaf patterns on plain paper. Duplicate the patterns on a copy machine, enlarging and reducing the scale at random and reversing the image. Make about 20 to 25 leaves using these leaf templates.

② Reserve about ⅛ yd. of two or three dark colors of wool jersey to use for leaf veins and stems, then machine-wash the remaining wool jersey pieces. Wash them at least once in hot water with no detergent, and dry them in a hot dryer. If you want the jersey to shrink even more and become thicker with more texture, wash them more than once. (The wool jersey can shrink as much as one-half the original width and length, so buy plenty. Every jersey shrinks differently, so wash samples first.)

③ For the wool jersey side of the afghan, cut the following sizes:
- Center: 36 in. by 51 in.
- Border A: 9 in. by 30 in.
- Border B: 9 in. by 31 in.
- Border C: 9 in. by 38 in.
- Border D: 9 in. by 6 in.
- Border E: 9 in. by 23 in.

Steps 1 and 2

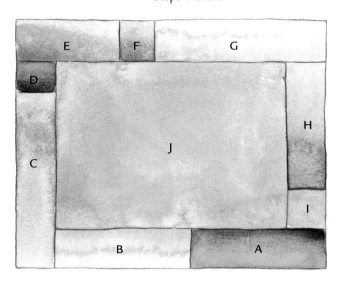

- Border F: 9 in. by 9 in.
- Border G: 9 in. by 38 in.
- Border H: 9 in. by 28 in.
- Border I: 9 in. by 10 in.

④ For the leaves, cut out generic shapes larger than the finished leaves from the small wool jersey scraps. Use a rotary cutter for a clean, straight edge.

⑤ For the other side of the afghan, cut one piece 53 in. by 68 in. from the leopard faux fur.

construction

① Following the illustration above, sew the border pieces together in the following order: A to B; C to D; E to F to G; and H to I. Sew each seam with a conventional ½-in. seam, then press open.

② Mark a ½-in. seam allowance around all sides of the center (J). Following the illustration above, sew each side border to the center in the following order: H/I to J; A/B to J; C/D to J; and E/F/G to J. Using an overlapping seam method, place the wrong side of the border on the right side of the center and stitch close to the cut edge.

Step 3

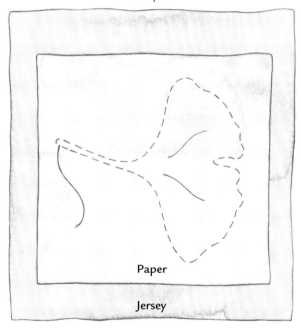

Paper

Jersey

Step 4

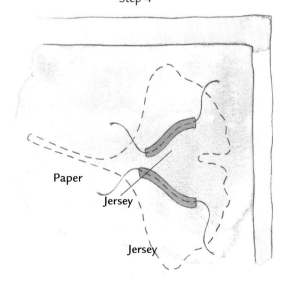

Paper

Jersey

Jersey

③ Place the leaf paper on top of the small scraps of wool jersey. Using black thread and a regular stitch length, stitch the outline of each leaf through the paper.

④ Using the reserved unwashed wool jersey, cut ½-in.-wide crossgrain strips of a few dark colors. Place the strips on the leaf veins, and stitch down the center through the paper, stretching the jersey as you sew. Remove the paper.

Step 6

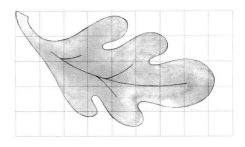

⑤ Remove the backing paper from the fusible adhesive, then following the manufacturer's directions, fuse the adhesive to the wrong side of each jersey scrap. Cut out each leaf using the black stitching line as a guide.

⑥ Following the schematic design of the afghan or creating your own design, arrange the leaves in a pleasing manner around the perimeter of the afghan. Remove the second paper backing from the adhesive, and fuse the leaves in place. If you feel that the leaves are likely to come loose with wear and tear on the afghan, stitch the leaves to the jersey following the first outline stitching.

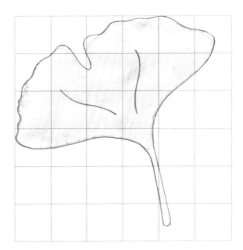

⑦ Where small leaves are in a cluster with stems, repeat step 4 to make connecting stems using wool jersey strips.

⑧ With right sides together, stitch the completed jersey side to the leopard faux fur, leaving an opening at one end. Turn the afghan to the outside and slipstitch the opening.

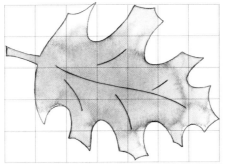

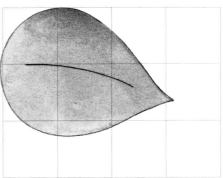

1 square = 1 inch

basket liner

> ## materials
>
> Fabric
>
> Lace
>
> Twill tape
>
> Decorative cord
>
> Thread to match

A LARGE-SCALE FLORAL PRINT fabric is used to make this simple basket liner. A long rectangle of fabric is sewn to a bottom circle. The outer edges are decorated with a vintage lace that conceals a casing through which decorative cord is tied. The finished size of this basket is 18 in. diameter by 12 in. high.

preparation

1 Measure the diameter of the bottom of the basket, then measure the circumference and the height.

2 Cut one piece of fabric the diameter of the bottom of the basket plus a $1/2$-in. seam allowance.

3 Cut one piece of fabric the length of the circumference of the bottom circle times $1^{1}/_{2}$. Add the turndown over the top of the basket (the sample was 8 in.) plus the casing width and two $1/2$-in. seam allowances to determine the width of the rectangle.

4 If the basket has handles, measure the width and determine the placement of them in the rectangle.

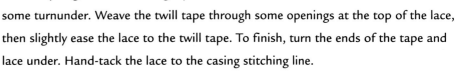

Step 1

⑤ From the lace, cut two pieces the same length as one-half of the circumference plus at least 10 in. for ease.

⑥ From the twill tape, cut two pieces the same length as the lace sections.

⑦ From the decorative cord, cut two pieces the same length as one-half of the circumference plus about 18 in. The amount of extra length to allow for the knot is determined by the diameter of the cord and how you want the tails to look. Allow enough extra, and cut off, if necessary.

construction

① Cut out the openings for the handles on the rectangle, then staystitch the inside corners of each cutout. Clip to each corner, turn under the seam allowances of the cutouts, and topstitch.

② Sew the short ends of the rectangle together, then finish the top edge of the rectangle. For the casing, turn the allowance under and topstitch. Leave the ends open where the handles intersect. If your basket does not have handles, make a continuous casing, leaving an opening to insert the cord.

Step 2

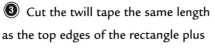

③ Cut the twill tape the same length as the top edges of the rectangle plus some turnunder. Weave the twill tape through some openings at the top of the lace, then slightly ease the lace to the twill tape. To finish, turn the ends of the tape and lace under. Hand-tack the lace to the casing stitching line.

④ Gather the other edge of the rectangle to fit the circumference of the circle and stitch.

Step 3

⑤ Insert the cording pieces into the casings, and tie the ends together in knots. Cut off the cord to the desired length, then wrap the ends with heavy thread, and fringe the ends of the cord.

Step 5

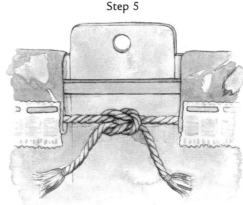

fringed pillow

Finished Size: 14 in. by 18 in.

THIS WESTERN-STYLE PILLOW has rows of cut and fringed faux suede. Alternating colors of camel and gray overlap one another. Rectangular in shape, the pillow is outlined in matching faux suede corded piping.

« m a t e r i a l s

$^2/_3$ yd. lightweight faux suede

$^1/_2$ yd. contrasting lightweight faux suede

$^1/_2$ yd. linen or duck cloth

Polyester thread to match

$^1/_8$-in.-wide double-faced basting tape

2 yd. cotton cable cord

One 14-in. by 18-in. down pillow form

Step 2

preparation

1 From the faux suede, cut 20 strips 1$^1/_2$ in. by 19 in. (cut 10 strips in the first color and 10 strips in the contrasting color). Use different directions of the nap to create color variations.

2 From the faux suede, cut one piece 15 in. by 19 in., and cut 2-in.-wide strips for the corded piping.

3 From the linen or duck cloth, cut one piece 15 in. by 19 in.

construction

1 Starting 1$^1/_2$ in. from one long edge, mark parallel lines $^3/_4$ in. apart on the linen or duck cloth.

2 Sew a line of stitching $^1/_2$ in. from the edge of each faux suede strip.

3 With small trimming scissors, cut fringe, using the stitching line as a guide to end the cut. Experiment with the width of fringe that you like. The sample pillow has $^1/_4$-in.-wide cuts.

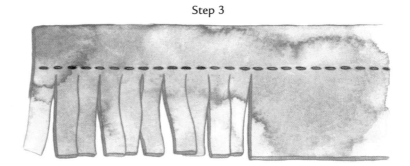

Step 3

Step 4

✳ It is easier to cut one or two sections of fringe out of the seam allowances before you assemble the pillow. Pin the remaining fringes on the first row out of the way so they won't get caught in the seam as you sew.

4 On the wrong side of each fringed strip, adhere the double-faced basting tape. Position the top of each strip on the marked lines, and press to hold in place. Stitch along the previous stitching and again at the top of the strip. Start with the bottom strip and sew before overlapping the next strip.

5 Make enough corded piping to go around the pillow. Sew the corded piping to the right side of the pillow, then trim fringe out of the seam allowances.

6 With right sides together, sew the front to the back, leaving an opening.

7 Turn the pillow to the outside, insert the pillow form, and slipstitch the opening.

laced pillow

A BEAUTIFUL PIECE OF TAPESTRY FABRIC is framed with mitered pieces of faux suede. The framework is sewn to the tapestry with wool jersey lacing. The back and corded piping are also faux suede.

FINISHED SIZE: 18 IN. BY 18 IN.

<< **materials**

½ yd. tapestry fabric

¾ yd. faux suede

⅛ yd. wool jersey

Temporary adhesive

Thread to match

2½ yd. cotton cable cord

One 18-in.-square down pillow form

preparation

1 From the tapestry fabric, cut one piece into a 12-in. square.

2 From the faux suede, cut four pieces 4 in. by 19 in., one piece into a 19-in. square, and two strips 2 in. wide by the width of the fabric.

3 From the wool jersey, cut four 1-in. by 18-in. strips.

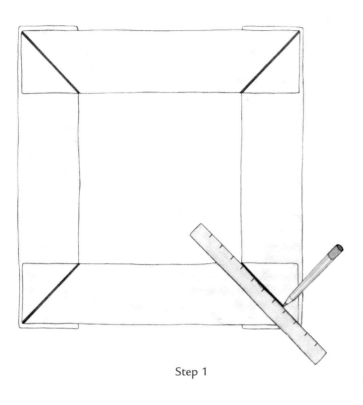

Step 1

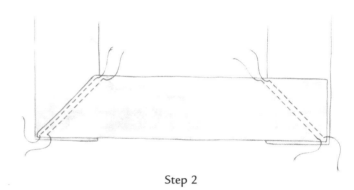

Step 2

construction

❶ Lay the four bands in a square, overlapping the corners, and pin. Draw diagonal lines at each corner.

❷ Stitch along each marked line, then stitch again ¼ in. away. Trim close to the second stitching.

Step 3

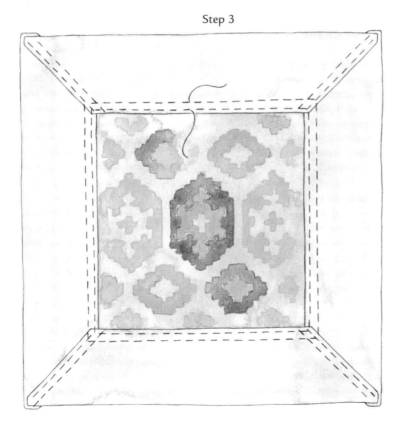

❸ Spray temporary adhesive around the edges of the tapestry square, then lay the faux suede frame over the tapestry center and press to hold in place. Topstitch next to the inner raw edge, and stitch again ¼ in. from the first stitching.

Step 4

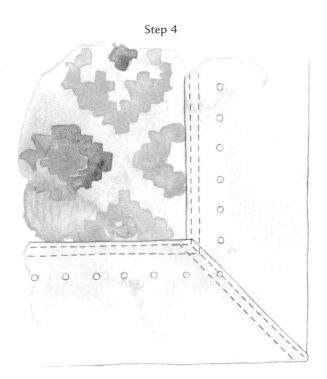

Step 5

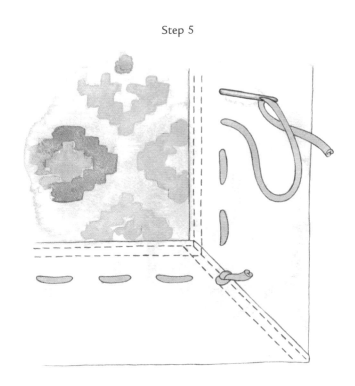

④ Using an awl and a hammer, punch holes through all layers along the inner edge of the frame about 1 in. from the edge and 1 in. apart.

⑤ Pin one end of a wool jersey strip to the ironing board, pull the other end, and steam the strip. The wool jersey will curl into a tube and remain that way when dry. Thread a carpet/tapestry needle with a steamed strip and "sew" through the punched holes. Begin and end the strip so that one knot shows on the surface of the pillow at each corner. The strip that ends on the wrong side can also be knotted. Sew all four sides of the frame.

⑥ Make enough faux suede corded piping to extend around all sides of the pillow, then sew the piping to the outer edge of the frame.

⑦ With right sides together, sew the pillow back to the front, leaving an opening. Turn the pillow to the outside, insert the form, and slipstitch the opening.

✱ If your sewing machine has problems sewing faux suedes, try using good-quality polyester thread, a jeans sharp or microfiber needle, and a regular stitch length. Double-sided basting tape can be used to hold the seam in place while sewing.

FINISHED SIZE: VARIABLE

mantel cover

« materials

Fabrics

- Tapestry fabric
- Animal print fabric or another
  fabric for the center section
- Plaid taffeta or another
  accent fabric

Cording

Lace

Temporary adhesive

Thread to match

THIS ELEGANT MANTEL COVER is designed to highlight the arabesque motif in the tapestry fabric. Part of the arabesque is cut out of the tapestry and appliquéd to a cotton animal print fabric and placed in the center of the cover. The plaid taffeta fabric is inserted not only to complete the dimensions of the piece but also to accent it. The bottom of the cover is embellished with heavy, hand-crocheted vintage lace. The finished cover is 77 in. wide by 12 in. deep by 16 in. high.

preparation

1 Measure the width and depth of the mantel, and determine the appropriate height of the cover.

2 Using the scaled illustration on the facing page as a general guide, make a paper pattern that works with your mantel size and with your fabric selection. Divide the pattern into sections that feature particular motifs, and balance it with the scale of your mantel. Place the pattern on your mantel to check the overall dimensions, then cut the pattern apart to use with each fabric.

3 From the tapestry fabric, cut out the tapestry sections, adding seam allowances. Use the pattern pieces at right.

4 From the animal print fabric, cut out the center section, adding seam allowances. Use the pattern from Step 2.

5 From the plaid taffeta, cut out the accent sections, adding seam allowances. Once again, use the pattern pieces from Step 2.

6 Cut bias strips of fabric that will be used to cover the cording. Sew them together in a continuous strip, if necessary.

7 From the cording, cut a length of cord that equals twice the width and depth of the cover plus the accent edges that will be corded.

8 From the lace, cut one piece equal to the length of the bottom of the cover plus turnback. Cut two pieces of lace equal to the depth of each end of the cover plus turnbacks.

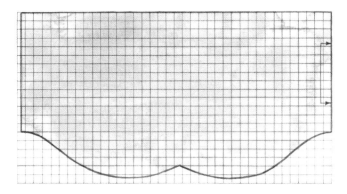

1 square = 1 inch

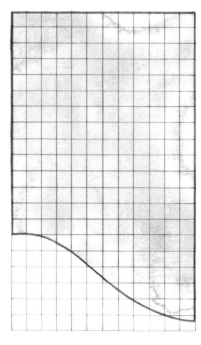

Step 2

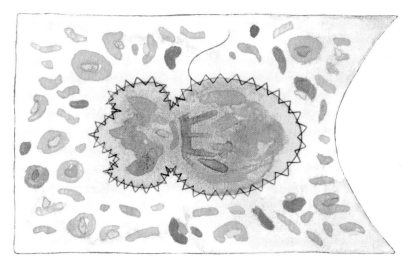

construction

1 Serge-finish all edges of the sections of the cover.

2 Select a motif from your tapestry fabric, then stitch around the outer edges of the motif and cut it out close to the stitching. Spray the back of the motif with temporary adhesive, and place it on the central section of the fabric. Using a zigzag stitch or blanket stitch, appliqué the motif to the fabric.

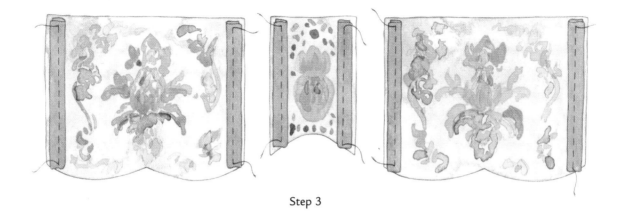

Step 3

3 Make enough covered corded piping to go around the top and to edge the plaid inserts. Sew the covered piping to both edges of the central fabric and to both edges of the front tapestry sections.

4 With right sides together, sew all front sections together.

5 Hem the sides of the front and ends.

6 Hand-sew the lace to the bottom of the front and ends, turning the ends under to finish.

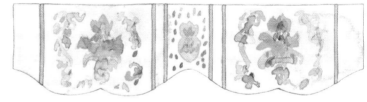

Step 4

7 Hem one long edge of the top piece, then sew the corded piping to the remaining three edges. Trim the inner cord from each end of the cording so that you can turn the ends to the wrong side to finish.

8 With right sides together, sew the front and ends to the top piece, pivoting at the corners.

Step 7

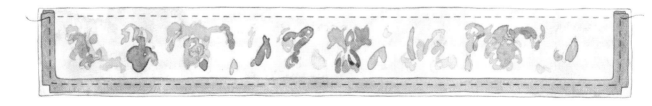

stenciled table cover

FINISHED SIZE: VARIABLE

THIS COARSELY WOVEN LINEN COVER for a square table consists of a top piece, four sides, and corner gussets. The bottom of each side panel is stenciled with a traditional ikat design, and the panels are tied together with wool jersey lacings through grommets. Wool jersey corded piping around the top and gussets coordinate with other projects in the room.

« materials

Fabric for the basic table cover

Contrasting wool jersey for the
    corner gussets and corded piping

24 metal grommets

Cotton cable cord

Stencil template
    (The one used in the sample is Aztec
    Border by Delta Technical Coatings;
    see Resources on p. 140)

Stencil sponge

Fabric paint
    (The paints used in the sample are
    Deka Cranberry Wine shadowed with
    Jaquard Metallic Textile Paint in
    metallic antique gold, metallic Aztec
    gold, brass, and black mixed with
    cranberry; see Resources on p. 140)

Thread to match

preparation

1 Measure the width, depth, and height of the table, and record the measurements.

2 For the basic table cover fabric, cut one piece of fabric the width and depth of the tabletop, adding ½-in. seam allowances on all four sides. Then cut four pieces of fabric the width of each side by the height of the table, adding a ½-in. seam allowance to the top edge and 1-in. hem allowances to the remaining three sides.

3 From the contrasting wool jersey fabric, cut 2-in.-wide crossgrain strips the length of the total width and depth of the tabletop. Piece the strips together, if necessary. Also, cut four gussets 8 in. wide by the height of the table, adding a ½-in. seam allowance to the top and a 1-in. hem allowance to the bottom. Finally, cut four 1-in.-wide strips at least 24 in. long.

Step 2

construction

1 Serge-finish all of the edges of all of the pieces. Using a chalk marker, mark 1-in. hem foldlines on all four side panels.

2 Using the Aztec Border stencil or the design of your choice, stencil the border pattern along the bottom of each side panel, keeping the design outside of the marked hemlines. Apply the foundation color with a dense sponge, then shade and layer color with a small stencil brush.

3 Turn the hems to the wrong sides of the three sides of each side panel and the side gussets. Miter the bottom corners (see pp. 134–135 for mitering instructions), then topstitch.

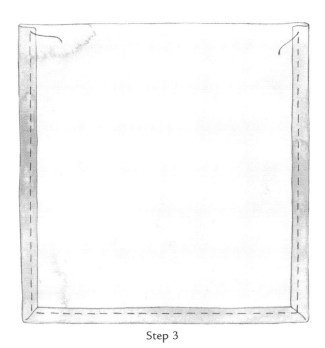

Step 3

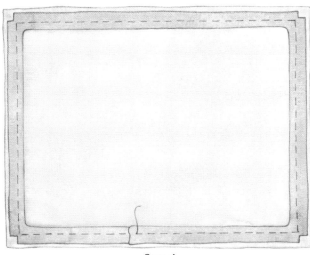

Step 4

4 Make enough corded piping to sew to all four sides of the tabletop.

5 With right sides together, pin each side to the top. Center the side gussets over each corner, then stitch through all layers.

Step 5

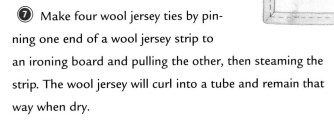

6 Install three grommets about 2½ in. apart, starting at the top of each side edge.

7 Make four wool jersey ties by pinning one end of a wool jersey strip to an ironing board and pulling the other, then steaming the strip. The wool jersey will curl into a tube and remain that way when dry.

8 Place the table cover on the table, then thread the jersey strip through the grommets like a shoelace. Tie in a knot at the end, and tie a knot in the end of each strip.

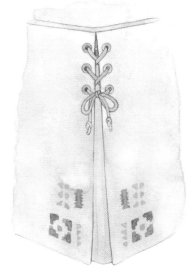

Step 8

the basics
for sewing

Any kind of sewing requires some basic equipment and sewing knowledge. In this chapter is a list and explanation of some equipment and skills that you need to create the projects in this book.

basic sewing equipment

Precision work requires good tools and the right equipment. The following essentials are recommended to have on hand for any sewing or craft project. Buy the best you can afford and add to your store of equipment often. Of course, the most important piece of equipment in your sewing space is a sewing machine that is a workhorse and performs perfectly. A serger is a wonderful accessory but not necessary in constructing the projects in this book. Find a space to work that has excellent light and adequate room to cut out and that, hopefully, will allow you to leave your project out when not working on it.

Tools for measuring and marking

Rulers, tapes, and other measuring devices provide the accuracy needed for exact cutting and consistent sewing. There are lots of marking tools on the market today. Test a few brands from each group and have several on hand for various fabric types.

Tape measure You'll need a narrow flexible tape from 60 in. to 120 in. long to measure large areas. It is useful to have the numbers marked on both sides with the numeral 1 at opposite ends.

Yardsticks and rulers Made of wood, plastic, or metal, large yardsticks are useful for measuring pieces of fabric, and smaller rulers aid in drawing or cutting along a solid edge for straight or bias cutting. A clear, plastic 2-in. by 18-in. ruler with a painted measurement grid is a popular size and shape for multiple uses.

T-square and L-square Typically made of metal or plastic, these squares are useful for measuring 45-degree and 90-degree angles and for finding and marking the lengthwise, crosswise, or bias grain on fabric.

45-degree right-angle triangle Used primarily for marking and cutting bias, these clear or colorful translucent plastic utensils are available in many sizes.

Seam gauge This 6-in. metal ruler has an adjustable marker and is handy for marking small measurements such as seam and hem allowances during construction.

Chalk markers Available in pencil, block, or powdered dispenser form, these tools highlight pertinent markings temporarily. Use white and light colors such as yellow or pale blue; avoid red. Use for free-form markings or next to a straightedge ruler on the right side of fabrics.

Erasable pens Marking pens in this category are either air-erasable or water-soluble with varying degrees of duration. Mark on the right or wrong side of fabric, but test its disappearing characteristics on a scrap first.

Tracing paper and tracing wheel Tracing paper is a waxy paper used in conjunction with a tracing wheel that transfers necessary markings to multiple layers of fabric. Purchase a good-quality paper whose markings will not fade away when ironed but will disappear when laundered or dry-cleaned. Test the paper first! Tracing wheels are available with smooth or serrated wheels. Generally, this type of marking equipment should not be used with sheer and delicate fabrics.

"Hera" marker This plastic or bone marker leaves an impression in the fabric with no residue or color remaining. It is perfect for silk, sheer, and other delicate fabrics.

Tools for cutting

As home sewing has become more professional, so have the tools for cutting. Where once we owned one pair of scissors for all purposes, there are now several choices as well as alternatives to scissors, depending on the fabric, the project, and the ease of use.

Scissors and shears Bent-handled shears in 8-in. or longer lengths cut fabric with the least number of strokes and with nice straight edges. Straight-handled scissors in 7-in. or shorter lengths are good for trimming, clipping, and grading. It is not unreasonable to expect to use three or four different kinds of scissors or shears in the construction of one project. Keep the blades sharp (have them sharpened by a professional).

Rotary cutter and cutting mat Sharp blades mounted in plastic housings make short work of cutting through multiple layers of fabrics from thin to thick. Rotary cutters are available in many shapes and sizes, some ergonomically designed, and the blades cut smoothly. Blades with novelty cutting designs are also available.

Seam ripper A fine-point ripper with a razor-sharp cutter delicately removes stitches without tearing the fabric. Some seam rippers even have a light at the end to illuminate fabrics sewn with dark thread. The finer and sharper, the better.

Weights To experiment with a layout or to cut out without pinning, weights hold tissue or fabric pattern pieces in place. Plastic-coated discs, painted whimsical metal objects, and fabric-covered pellet tubes are just some of the varieties available.

Tools for sewing

The most important piece of equipment in your sewing space is, of course, a sewing machine that is a workhorse and performs perfectly. A serger is a wonderful accessory to have, but it's not necessary in constructing the projects in this book. Having the right collection of presser feet (see the sidebar below) and other sewing aids simplifies your tasks and adds to the pleasure of it all.

Pins Fresh, good-quality pins are important. Throw away your tired pins and buy new glass-head silk pins. The glass heads are easy to pick up and will not melt near heat; their fine points will not damage better fabrics.

Needles Needles are much like pins—they need to be fine and extra sharp. For hand-sewing, look for good-quality Japanese or English needles with eyes that are easy enough for you to thread. For machine-sewing, keep a good supply of standard needles in all sizes from 60/8 to 90/14. Other specialty needles to have on hand include topstitching (110/18), jeans sharps for extra-fine fabrics, microtex for unusual fabrics and the new synthetics, metafil for metallic threads, and leather needles

special presser feet

The standard presser feet that come with your machine are the primary feet needed to make the projects in this book. But newly designed specialty feet aid in the sewing process, improve your technical skills, and, in some cases, speed the process.

Edgestitch foot

The metal guide blade of this foot allows you to stitch a straight line close to an edge with little trouble.

Embroidery foot

This foot has an open toe to aid in seeing decorative stitches as they are sewn and to follow premarked motifs easily.

Hemming foot

Fabric is automatically rolled into the edges of this foot to create perfect rolled hems. There are several widths to choose from. This foot takes practice before starting in on a final project.

Patchwork foot

When you want a perfect 1/4-in. seam or hem, the width of this foot helps you to execute it with precision. Notches engraved on the toe of the foot indicate when to turn a corner exactly 1/4 in. from the end.

Walking foot

Sometimes called an even-feed foot, this foot allows the top layer of fabric to feed through the sewing machine at the same speed as the bottom layer and prevents fabric creep. This is especially useful when sewing velvet and other pile fabrics and for matching plaids.

for real and faux suedes and leathers. Change the needle for every fabric type and after every project.

Beeswax Passing a strand of thread through a cake of beeswax and melding the wax into the thread with heat (using an iron) prevents tangling and knotting and adds strength.

Sewing machine You don't need a fancy machine with lots of extra stitches and features to make the projects in this book, but it is important to have a reliable machine with a good-quality stitch that sews on a variety of fabric thicknesses and weights and sews with many kinds of thread, including decorative.

Serger A serger is certainly nice to have, but it is not essential for home-decorating sewing. A serger should overlock a very flat, medium-wide three- or four-thread stitch formation with perfection on all types of fabrics from chiffon to wool. A differential (the ability to alter the upper and lower fabric feeding) is essential.

Embroidery machine While not essential, an embroidery machine is necessary for the embroidery motif on the linen napkins in chapter 3. Also, if you really like embroidery, you can substitute an embroidery motif for the stenciling on the table cover in chapter 4. Obviously, you can leave the embroidery off these projects, but if you have an embroidery machine, you can copy the motifs just as they are or you can personalize your projects with your own design.

Tools for pressing

To produce professional-looking projects, it's essential to develop good pressing skills. Use the right equipment for the task and the fabric, and press frequently throughout the construction process.

Iron Just as a sewing machine needs to be reliable, so does an iron. Look for a properly weighted iron with a cleanable sole plate, multiple levels of dry or moist heat, and lots of steam when you want it. This is one time when the more expensive the iron the better the quality.

Press cloths Using a press cloth helps to prevent fabric shine, scorching, and iron marks. The fabric dictates the type of press cloth—sheer cotton/poly for delicate and fine fabrics, heavier duck-type cloth for heavy fabrics. Always test your iron on the fabric before beginning the construction.

Templates Lightweight cardboard such as tagboard can be cut into shapes to use as pressing templates. For hems, cut a 2-in. by 18-in. piece and draw horizontal lines in ¼-in. increments. Place the template on the wrong side of the fabric. Bring the raw edge of the fabric up and over the straight edge of the template, aligning it with a marked line the same width as the finished hem, and press through all layers. Templates can be any shape (curves, points, straight edges) to ensure precision pressing, especially in slippery fabrics.

Clapper When placed over a steamed section of fabric, this hardwood block will help to remove the moisture from the fabric quickly. A clapper also aids in pressing a seam or edge more crisply.

Point presser Small, trimmed seam allowances are best pressed open first over a narrow strip of wood with a pointed end before turning the seam to the inside. Point pressers are sometimes mounted on a clapper for a two-in-one piece of equipment.

Sleeve board A sleeve board is a two-level padded surface shaped like a small ironing board that's useful for pressing seams and other details in a tube. It prevents unwanted press marks where the fabric folds and where the iron is wider than the fabric strip.

pressing surfaces for pile fabrics

To avoid marring, iron impressions, and other damage, special surfaces are necessary when pressing velvet and other pile fabrics.

Velvaboard—a dense, deep-pile "fabric" that cushions the fabric being pressed.

Needle board—a bed of steel needles with the ultimate protection value.

Industrial needle board—a large sheet of the sticky side of hook-and-loop tape that is flexible for pressing curved or shaped seams.

Turkish towel—the most accessible at home is a fluffy towel.

a glossary of stitches

You need to have a repertoire of stitches, both machine and hand, to handle fabrics effectively. Take the time to learn how and when to use them. It's worth it!

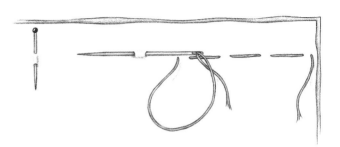

Basting

Basting is a temporary stitch either by hand or machine used to prepare seams and other details and to hold the fabric in place until permanent stitching can be done. Remove the basting thread before pressing or use silk thread, which does not leave a mark when pressed. Always baste just inside the permanent stitching line. Hand-basting stitches include the following:

Even basting Even basting is generally used for long seams and in areas that are stressed and need to be controlled. Space stitches evenly, ¼ in. long and ¼ in. apart, beginning and ending with a backstitch rather than a knot.

Diagonal basting Diagonal basting is used to hold fabrics together that are difficult to work with and tend to creep, such as velvet, corduroy, and slippery silks and satins. Take short stitches through the fabric at a right angle to the edge, spacing them evenly. You will see diagonal stitches on the top and short, horizontal stitches on the underside.

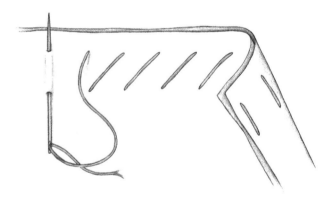

Chainstitch (thread chain)

A chainstitch, or thread stitch, is a series of looped and interlaced stitches linked to form a thick, secure thread. Securely fasten a double thread to the fabric with one or two overlapping stitches. Form a loop on the right side by taking another short stitch. Slip the thumb and first two fingers of your left hand through the loop while holding the needle and thread end in your right

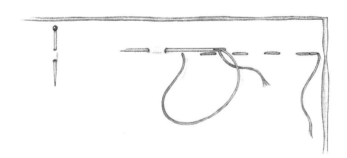

Uneven basting Uneven basting is used for marking and for holding fabric together that's not stressed, such as a hem. Take a long stitch on the top surface and a shorter stitch through the fabric.

hand **(a)**. Using the second finger of your left hand, pick up a new loop and pull it through the first loop **(b)**, tightening the loop as you proceed **(c)**. Continue to work the chain to the desired length. Secure the free end with several small stitches **(d)**.

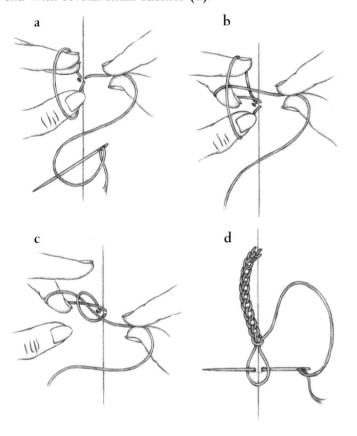

a   b

c   d

Edgestitch

This is a line of stitching an even distance from a folded or creased edge. It holds an edge in place and adds a decorative element.

Finish

This term refers to a variety of methods used to neaten an edge when it's not enclosed. Common finishes are serged (overlocked), zigzagged, pinked, turned and stitched, and bound with bias tape, fabric, or Seams Great bias mesh tape.

Half backstitch

This stitch is used to understitch seams to prevent edges from rolling toward the outside. Bring the needle through the fabric to the upper side. Take a stitch back about ⅛ in., bringing the needle out again ¼ in. from the beginning of the first stitch. Take another stitch ⅛ in. and continue in the same manner.

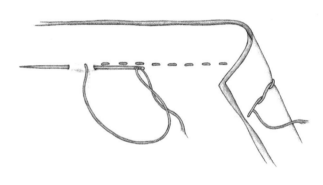

Prickstitch

This variation of a backstitch is a hand stitch commonly used to insert a zipper, but it produces a decorative stitch as well. Carry the needle back only one or two threads (or any desired distance), forming a tiny surface stitch with a reinforced understitch.

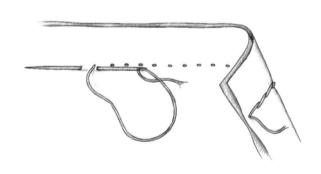

Slipstitch

This invisible hand stitch is used to hem, hold trims in place, and close openings. Slide the needle through the folded edge and at the same point pick up a thread of the under fabric. Continue in this manner, taking stitches ⅛ in. to ¼ in. apart and spacing the stitches evenly.

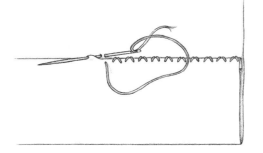

Tailor's tacks

This method of marking through a single or double layer of fabric is used when other methods of marking would mar the fabric and when working with soft-surfaced fabrics such as velvet. Using a double strand of thread without a knot, take a single small running stitch

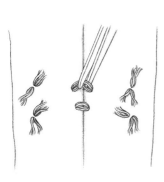

through the fabric. Then sew another stitch across the first, pulling the thread until a large loop is formed. Gently roll the top layer of fabric back, and cut the threads between the layers, leaving tufts on either side.

Topstitching

Topstitching is sewn on the right side of the fabric and is meant to be decorative, whether subtle or dominant. Thicker threads in interesting fibers such as rayon can be used in tandem with special needle sizes.

Understitch

When a seamline is pressed to form an edge that encloses the seam allowances, the underside should be understitched. Press the trimmed seam allowances to one side. From the right side, half-backstitch or machine-stitch close to the seamline and through all the seam allowances.

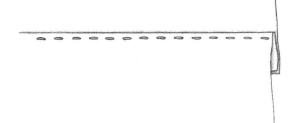

fabric preparation

Each fabric selected for your project should be studied carefully. Know the fiber content, learn about the care of the fabric, and understand the use of the final piece so that you can prepare your fabric accordingly.

Preshrinking

It is always a good idea to preshrink fabric before you cut it out. In the case of the home-decorating projects in this book, pretreat the fabric in the same manner that you will clean the finished item. Laundering, dry-cleaning, and steaming are the methods used to prepare fabrics. Most fabrics can be laundered either by hand or machine, even those that are traditionally dry-cleaned such as silk, wool, and velvet. Experiment with a scrap of fabric first. Many times, simply heavily steaming a piece of fabric will emulate dry-cleaning without the expense.

Straight of grain

Many times the success or failure of a sewing project is directly related to whether the fabric has the correct grain, which means that the crosswise and lengthwise threads are at perfect right angles to each other. To check the grainline, the true crossgrain needs to be established. This can be done by tearing the fabric if it is a natural fiber or by pulling and removing a crosswise thread and cutting along the resulting space. Fold the fabric lengthwise, matching selvages and the fabric ends. If the edges do not align on all three sides, the fabric is off-grain and must be straightened.

Fabric can be straightened by steam-pressing the threads into proper alignment. With the fabric folded lengthwise, right sides together, pin every 5 in. to a padded surface such as a blocking board or ironing board along the selvages and ends. Press firmly, stroking from the selvages toward the fold.

Another method is to pull the fabric gently but firmly in the opposite direction from the way the ends slant until a perfect right-angle corner is formed. Sometimes a combination of the two methods can be used.

construction techniques

Construction techniques for home-decorating projects are the same or similar to the techniques used in garment sewing. Following is a review of some of the most common techniques.

Hems and edges

Hems and edges define the look of a project, from casual to formal, and edges should be finished for long-term wear. Although raw edges have their place in today's design, it is generally considered preferable to enclose raw edges and finish them by hand or machine.

special handling of sheer fabrics

Sheer fabrics such as chiffon and georgette and other opaque silk fabrics require special techniques and materials when cutting out to ensure that they will hang on the straight of grain. Because they are so slippery, they need to be held in place and not allowed to move all over your cutting table.

Cover the cutting surface with white paper that's gritty on one side and smooth on the other (such as examining-room paper). Lay a single layer of fabric on top of the paper, aligning the selvage with the long edge of the paper and the torn or cut edges with the ends of the paper. Staple or pin every few inches all of the edges of the fabric to the paper. Use a chalk marker to determine the cutting lines. Use microserrated scissors to cut through both the fabric and paper. These specialized scissors grab the fabric and inhibit the fabric creeping away from you as you cut. Mark each piece with tailor's tacks or with a Hera marker before removing the fabric from the table.

Handkerchief hem (narrow hem) Use this hem on cotton and linen and other crisp fabrics. Turn ¼ in. to the wrong side and press. Turn up edge again and press. Stitch by machine through all thicknesses.

Baby hem Use this hem on delicate and fine fabrics such as silk, chiffon, and georgette. Staystitch ⅜ in. from the raw edge. Turn ⅜ in. to the wrong side along the staystitching line, and edgestitch next to the folded edge. Using small trimming scissors or appliqué scissors, trim the excess fabric close to the stitching. Turn the edge up again and edgestitch. The finished hem is approximately ⅛ in. wide.

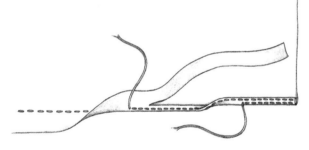

Rolled hems

By hand—Machine-stitch ¼ in. from the raw edge, and trim close to the stitching. Roll approximately ⅛ in. of the edge between your thumb and forefinger, concealing the stitching. Stabilize the roll with your third and fourth fingers and slipstitch, taking a single thread at each stitch. This is considered a couture edge.

By machine—Most sewing machines have special presser feet that allow a fabric edge to feed through a cone-shaped section, rolling the fabric and stitching it down at the same time.

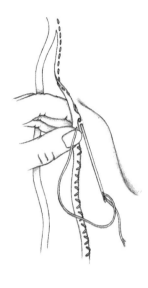

By serging—Many sergers have the added feature of rolling an edge and overcasting it with either two or three threads.

Seams

Standard seam allowances used for the projects in this book are ½ in. wide unless otherwise noted.

Trimming Seam allowances should be trimmed only where less bulk is desired. For an enclosed seam, seam allowances should be trimmed to ¼ in. When two seams intersect at a right angle or at other corners, trim diagonally.

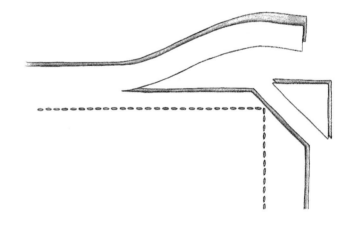

Grading When seam allowances are enclosed and turned together, trim each layer a different width to reduce bulk.

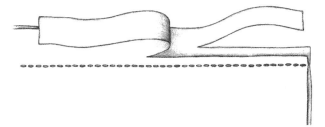

Clipping Curved seams require special trimming and clipping in order to lie flat. Trim an outward curve to ⅛ in. On an inside curve, clip into the seam allowance at even intervals. The tighter the curve, the closer the clips.

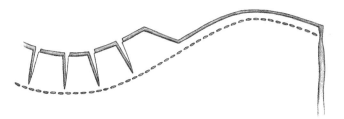

Intersecting seams Special sewing and trimming techniques are necessary when two seams cross. Stitch one seam and press open. Stitch the second seam in the same manner. Pin the two seams with right sides together, using a pin point to match the crossed seams exactly at the seamline. Then pin on either side of the seams and stitch. Trim corners diagonally.

Guides for sewing straight seams Mark the seamline with a line of chalk and stitch over the marking. Hold the fabric taut behind the presser foot with one hand, and guide the fabric in front of the presser foot with the other hand.

Attach a magnetic seam guide to the throat of your sewing machine, and align the edge of the fabric with the guide edge.

French seam This enclosed seam looks like a plain seam on the right side and a small tuck on the wrong side. With wrong sides together, stitch ⅜ in. from the seamline in the seam allowance. Trim to ⅛ in. With right sides together, stitch along the seamline (¼ in. from the creased seam), encasing the raw edges.

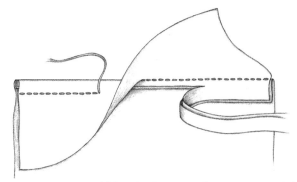

Flat-fell seam A self-finished seam, this version of the flat-fell seam can be completed without the use of a sewing-machine felling foot. Press one-half of the seam allowance to the right side (**a**). Trim one-half of the seam allowance away from the other side of the seam (**b**). With right sides together, position the trimmed

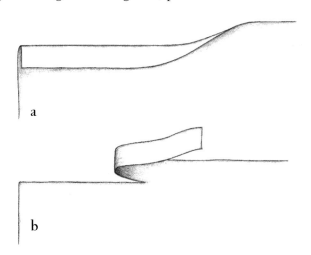

a

b

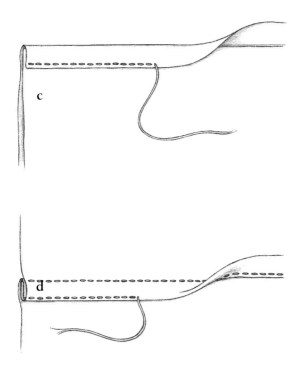

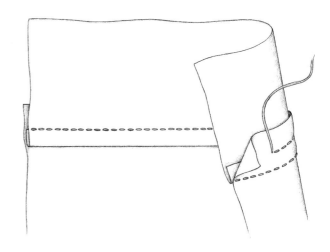

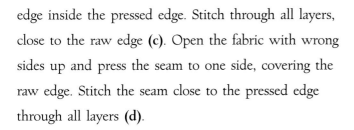

edge inside the pressed edge. Stitch through all layers, close to the raw edge **(c)**. Open the fabric with wrong sides up and press the seam to one side, covering the raw edge. Stitch the seam close to the pressed edge through all layers **(d)**.

Mock flat-fell seam This method creates a look of a traditional flat-fell seam but is easier to sew. Sew a standard seam with the rights sides together. Trim one side of the seam allowance to about ¼ in., then press the seam to one side, covering the trimmed edge. Topstitch ¼ in. from the seam through all layers.

Corners

Carefully crafted corners mark the difference between professional and homemade. Use sound techniques to sew precision corners.

Reinforcing a corner seam When stitching a straight piece of fabric to a corner, first staystitch through the portion of the seam that will need to turn the corner. Clip to the point. With right sides together, pin both sections with the clipped section up and stitch, pivoting at the point.

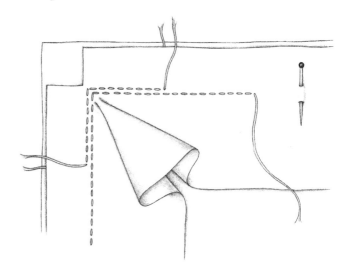

Right-angled corner When joining two corresponding pieces of fabric, shorten the stitch length for about 1 in. on either side of the corner.

Acute-angled corners If the corner is at an acute angle, take one or two small stitches across the point, depending on the weight of the fabric.

Piped seams

Seams and edges become more defined and interesting when decorative piping is inserted.

Right-angled corner Baste piping to the right side of the fabric along the seamline, matching raw edges. Clip through the flange to the cording at the corner. Stitch, pivoting at the clipped corner.

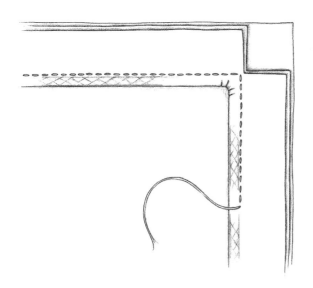

sewing specialty fabrics

The luxurious fabrics of today and the innovative weaves and blends of fibers require special skills and tools to produce professional results.

Velvet
Sewing two pieces of velvet together is difficult, but sewing one layer of velvet to a smooth fabric is even more challenging. Slippage and creeping are common problems. Some tricks that will reduce frustration include knowing that you need to baste, baste, baste. Diagonal basting using silk thread is the best method. Use a walking foot, roller foot, or Teflon foot and sew in the direction of the nap. You may need to decrease the pressure on the presser foot and hold the fabric taut while stitching. Match the weight of the thread to the weight of the fabric. You may need to use embroidery-weight cotton thread or 100% silk thread.

Silks and sheers
Slippery fabrics such as chiffon, crepe de Chine, georgette, charmeuse, and even some fine rayons require special handing. Some basting may be required, but more important, use good-quality sharp needles in small sizes such as 60/8, 65/10, or 70/12. Buy good-quality thread (100% cotton embroidery or 100% silk), reduce your stitch length, and hold the fabric taut while sewing. A product called Perfect Sew can be used to stabilize the stitching lines as long as you are willing to launder the fabric to remove it after sewing.

Curve Stitch the piping to the right side of the fabric, matching the raw edges. Clip through the flange to the cording at regular intervals to allow the piping to fit the curve smoothly.

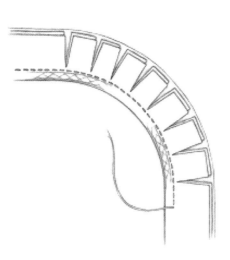

Miters

Sewing a miter on an outside corner is the cleanest way to finish an edge. There is also less bulk than an ordinary folded corner.

Square corners Turn all seam or hem allowances to the inside and press **(a)**. At the corner, open the seam or hem allowances and turn to the inside diagonally across the point and press **(b)**. With right sides together, stitch through the diagonal line. Trim to ¼ in. **(c)**. Press the seam open over a point presser **(d)**. Turn to the outside, press, and topstitch **(e)**.

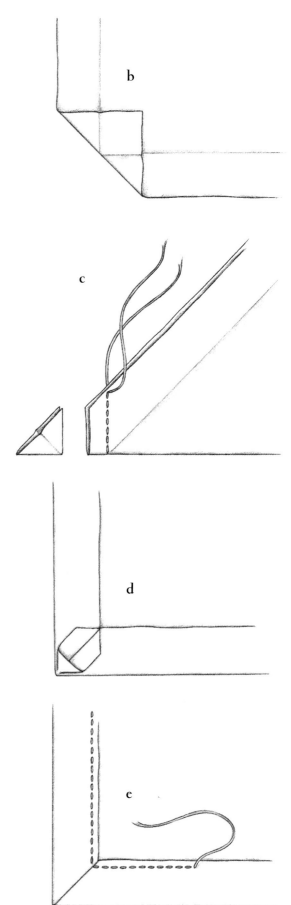

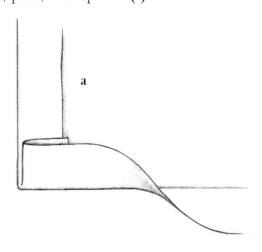

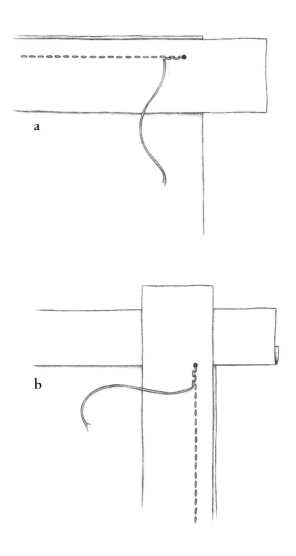

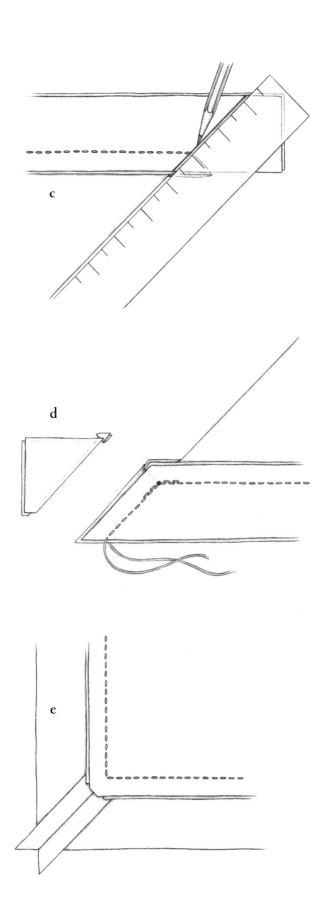

Single-faced band With right sides together, stitch a ½-in. seam starting and stopping stitching ½ in. from each end **(a)**. Press the band away from the center. Stitch the adjacent band to the edge starting at the seam of the previous band and ending ½ in. from the other end **(b)**. Fold diagonally through the corner, matching raw edges. Draw a diagonal line on the band, extending the line formed by the fold of the center **(c)**. Stitch on the marked line, starting at the previous stitching and taking care not to catch the seam allowances **(d)**. Trim the ends of the band ½ in. from the stitching. Press the miter seam allowances open **(e)**. Press the remaining seam allowances toward the band.

Double-faced band Begin by cutting a strip of fabric four times the finished width of the band. Press the strip in half lengthwise, then press each raw edge to the center crease line **(a)**. With right sides together, align the raw edges and stitch along the first crease line **(b)**. End the stitching at a point that equals the finished width of the band, then backstitch. At the ending point of the stitch, diagonally fold the band away from the edge at a right angle, then fold the band straight down,

matching the fold to the two raw edges and aligning the other raw edges **(c)**.

Keeping the opposite raw edge folded to the center crease, draw an arrow from the previous stitch ending point diagonally to the center crease folded edge and back down to the opposite edge, parallel with the starting point. Stitch along the marked line through the band only. Continue stitching the band to the project along the first crease line **(d)**. Turn the band to the underside, and slipstitch the folded edge to the seam-allowance stitching line **(e)**. You may need to do some trimming, depending on the bulk of the fabric.

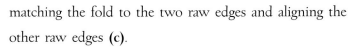

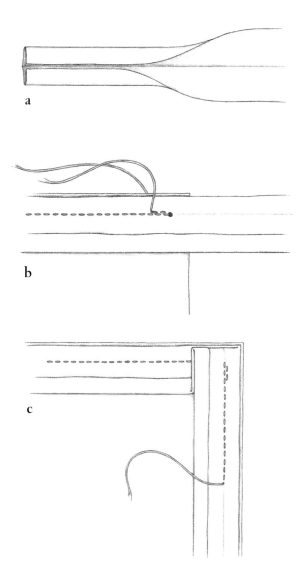

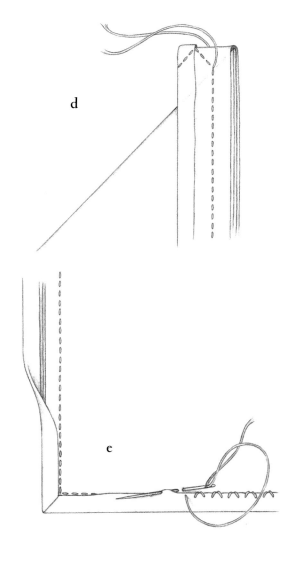

Bias binding

Binding is a beautiful way to finish an edge. Bindings can blend or accent an edge. They are cut on the bias so they will lie smooth around curves and corners.

Cutting bias Using a rectangular piece of fabric, fold it diagonally at one end to find the true bias. Using the bias fold as a guideline, mark parallel lines the desired width, allowing a ¼-in. seam allowance. Piecing the strips together is done in one of two ways:

Continuous pieced strips—On the marked piece of fabric, join the shorter ends, right sides together, with one strip width extending beyond the edge at each side **(a)**. Stitch a ¼-in. seam and press open **(b)**. Begin cutting on the marked line at one end, and continue in a circular fashion **(c)**.

Individual pieced strips—Cut along the markings for the bias strips. With right sides together, match the seamlines of the short diagonal ends and stitch **(a)**. Press the seam open **(b)**.

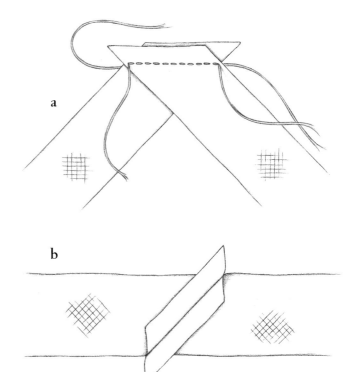

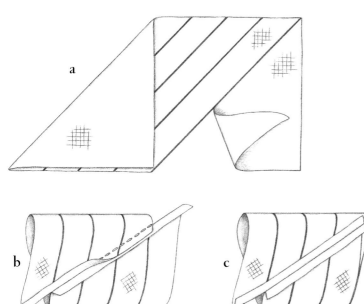

Single binding Cut bias strips four times the finished width plus ¼ in. to ⅜ in. Press in half lengthwise, and press the raw edges to the center crease line. Open out and, matching raw edges, stitch along the seamline **(a)**. Turn the bias over the seam allowance and slipstitch over the seamline **(b)**.

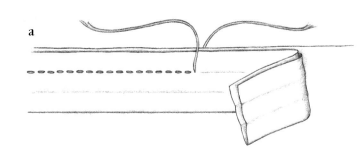

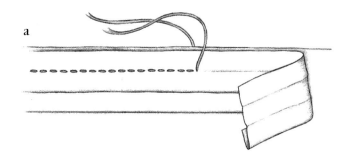

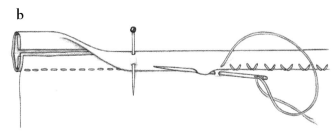

Joining binding

A single or double binding is joined by stopping your stitching slightly before reaching an area of the joining. Open out the strip and fold the fabric so the strip ends are at right angles. Stitch the ends close to the fabric but without catching the fabric in the stitching. Trim the seam allowances to ¼ in. and press open. Finish stitching the strip to the fabric across the joining.

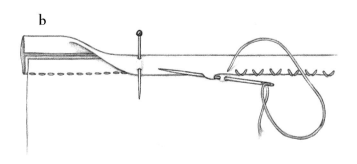

Double binding (French) Cut bias strips six times the finished width plus ¼ in. to ⅜ in. Fold the strip in half lengthwise with wrong sides together and press. Matching raw edges, stitch the bias to the right side of the fabric along the seamline **(a)**. Turn the strip over the seamline and slipstitch in place **(b)**. If the bias has been cut slightly wider, the bias can be completed by machine-stitching in the well of the seam and catching the folded edge on the underside.

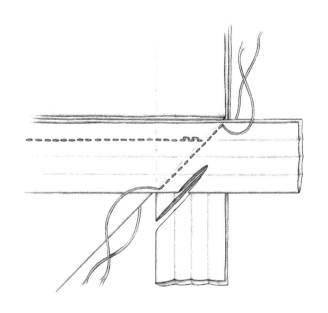

Lining and underlining

When is it necessary to change the performance of a fabric—to add weight and drape, conceal raw edges, or add an accent color or texture—lining or underlining techniques are useful.

Lining Lining gives a project a quality finished look. A lining prolongs the life of the piece and hides the inner construction details. It prevents stretching, helps preserve the shape, reduces wrinkling, and adds body to limp fabrics. Linings are sometimes meant to show, such as in curtains, so some thought needs to be given to the color, texture, and weight of the fabric chosen. The same fabric as the fashion fabric may be selected, or the fabric may be contrasting, patterned, sheer, or simply outrageous.

Underlining Underlining fabrics are cut to the same size as the outer fashion fabric pieces. Then the underlining and fashion fabric are basted and sewn together to act as one layer throughout the construction. Underlining adds body and durability by supporting and reinforcing the fabric and seams. It helps to reduce wrinkling and prevent stretching. Some underlinings alter the overall effect of the outer fabric, adding richness and visual weight. Some suggestions for underlinings include batiste, China silk, organza, muslin, taffeta, and flannel.

working with fabrics

Heavy fabric

When working on home-decorating projects, it is common to use heavyweight, upholstery-type fabrics. Your sewing machine needs to be in good working order, clean, and oiled. Change to a larger needle, at least a 90/14mm, and learn to hold the fabric taut with both hands as you guide the fabric through the sewing machine.

Large amounts of fabrics

You will need to have sufficient working space while working with large amounts of fabric. In addition to a large amount of "lay-off" table space as part of your sewing-machine table, add another table either to the left or behind your machine so that the fabric does not fall to the floor too close to your machine. You may need to move your sewing machine away from a wall or corner to allow space to manipulate your project.

Resources

Fabric Retailers

Ah! Kimono
16004 NE 195th St.
Woodinville, WA 98072-6459
(425) 482-6485; (425) 486-6797,
(425) 482-6487 FAX
www.ahkimono.com
Kimono fabrics

Calico Corners
Call (800) 213-6366 for the store
nearest you
www.calicocorners.com
Decorator fabrics, down jumbo bed rolls

Jo-Ann Stores Inc.
5555 Darrow Rd.
Hudson, OH 44236
(330) 656-2600
www.joann.com
*Cotton batting, cambric dust covers, cardboard
tack strips*

Kasuri Dyeworks
1959 Shattuck Ave.
Berkeley, CA 94704
(510) 841-4509
Kimono fabrics

Mendels Far Out Fabrics
1556 Haight St.
San Francisco, CA 94117
(415) 621-1287
Clipped-weave Indian cotton

Nell Hill's
501 Commercial
Atchison, KS 66002
(913) 367-1086
www.nellhills.com
Cotton tapestry

The Rain Shed
707 N.W. 11th St.
Corvallis, OR 97330
(514) 753-8900

Satin Moon Fabrics
32 Clement St.
San Francisco, CA 94118
(415) 668-1623

Thai Silks
252 State St.
Los Altos, CA 94022
(650) 948-8611
www.thaisilks.com
Silk dupioni and organza

Threadwear
2236 SW Oakley Ave.
Topeka, KS 66604
(785) 235-1552
www.sewingworkshop.com
Clipped-weave Indian cotton, silk dupioni, organza

Fabric Manufacturers

Brunschwig & Fils
75 Virginia Rd.
N. White Plains, NY 10603
(914) 684-5800
Silk taffeta

M&A Linens, Inc.
270 W. 39th St., 10th floor
New York, NY 10018
(212) 869-5078
Linen

Scalamandre
300 Trade Zone Dr.
Ronkonkoma, NY 11779
(516) 467-8800
Historical reproduction prints

F. Schumacher & Co.
1325 Old Cooch's Bridge Rd.
P. O. Box 6002
Newark, DE 19714
(800) 523-1200
Silk matelassé

Grosgrain Ribbon

Britex
146 Geary St.
San Francisco, CA 94108
(415) 392-2910

Elsie's Exquisites
Karen Snyder
P. O. Box 7177
Laguna Miguel, CA 92607
(949) 831-3781
www.festivegiftwrap.com
List of retailers for Mokuba ribbon

JKM Products Inc.
431 Commerce Ln., Unit B
West Berlin, NJ 08091
(609) 767-6604
(609) 767-7572 FAX
Jkmproducts@aol.com
Mokuba ribbon by mail order

Mokuba Ribbon
561 7th Ave.
New York, NY 10018
(212) 302-5010

Ruban Et Fleur
8655 S. Sepulveda Blvd.
Los Angeles, CA 90045
(310) 641-3466

Potpourri

Agraria
1050 Howard St.
San Francisco, CA 94103
(800) 824-3632

Caswell-Massey Co., Ltd.
518 Lexington Ave.
New York, NY 10017
(212) 755-2254

Miscellaneous Supplies

Chambers
3250 Van Ness Ave.
San Francisco, CA 94109
(800) 334-9790
Catalog, down bolster pillows

The Company Store
500 Company Store Rd.
La Crosse, WI 54601
(800) 285-3606
Catalog, bolster pillow forms, bed roll forms

Cuddledown of Maine
312 Canco Rd.
Portland, ME 04103
(800) 323-6793
Lap quilts

Garnet Hill
231 Main St.
Franconia, NH 03580-0262
(800) 622-6216
*Catalog, down pillow forms, down boudoir pillow
forms*

Pat Mahoney
537 York St.
P. O. Box 335
Lodi, CA 95241
(209) 369-5410
Covered buttons

Manny's Millinery Supply Center
63 W. 38th St.
New York, NY 10018
(212) 840-2235
(212) 944-0178 FAX
*Retail, wholesale, mail order; hat bodies, trims,
tools, horsehair, buckram hat forms, rayon grosgrain
ribbon; catalog $3; $25 minimum for mail order*

Personal FX
P. O. Box 664
Moss Beach, CA 94038
(800) 482-6066
Beads and findings

Sew Fancy
Beverly Johnson & Mary Ellen Timperon
171 Lees Ave., Suite 1703
Ottawa, Ontario, Canada K1S 5P3
(905) 775-1396
Drapery supplies

Things Japanese
9805 N.E. 116th St., Suite 7160
Kirkland, WA 98034
(206) 821-2287
Silk thread

H. Lynn White
8208 Nieman Rd.
Lenexa, KS 66214
(800) 999-4483
*Manufacturer of trims, bullion fringe, loop fringe,
rosettes, tassels; call for the nearest distributor or
retailer*